Winning with Past Performance

Strategies for Industry and Government

Winning with Past Performance

Strategies for Industry and Government

Jim Hiles
W. Earl Wells

MANAGEMENTCONCEPTSPRESS

𝗜𝗜𝗜

MANAGEMENTCONCEPTS PRESS

8230 Leesburg Pike, Suite 800
Tysons Corner, VA 22182
(703) 790-9595
Fax: (703) 790-1371
www.managementconcepts.com

Library of Congress Control Number: 2014941983

ISBN: 978-1-56726-466-1
eISBN: 978-1-56726-449-4

ABOUT THE AUTHORS

Jim Hiles started with past performance as a contracting official choosing between competing offerors. He retired after a distinguished career in the U.S. Navy and subsequently led organizational development initiatives at multiple companies, developing and refining contract, partner/vendor management, business development, and service delivery functions.

Earl Wells started with past performance management as a proposal manager for Electronic Data System's government services division. Since then he has been a capture, proposal, and operations manager for government services at firms including Systemhouse, PRC, Oracle, and BlackBox. Earl has been a Shipley Associates proposal consultant and currently works with multiple companies as a founding partner of Kapner-Wells Consulting.

CONTENTS

FOREWORD

The past should not be where we're heading. But it discloses where we've been and tells us how we've performed. And that performance can measure our likely success in the future.

One of my mantras is that for contractors to be successful in the federal marketplace, they must have an unrelenting focus on "performance, performance, performance." But even federal contracting firms that think they have performed with excellence must ask: *If no one knows about it, did it really happen?*

The answer is that past performance is their opportunity to make sure people know about it. In the federal marketplace, there is an almost continuous expansion of federal regulations, agency initiatives, and contracting officer trainings focused on measuring contractor performance, reporting on that performance in a consistent and timely manner, and evaluating those past performance reports for future source selection decisions. Government contractors must pay close attention to their past performance record or else pay another price—in the form of exclusion from future awards.

For those who are serious about managing and leveraging their past performance portfolio, *Winning with Past Performance* is a must-read. It provides both the *what* and the *how* to use past performance information successfully in future opportunities. I'm not aware of any single book that compares to this one, for the full spectrum analysis of issues relating to past performance in the federal marketplace that Jim Hiles and Earl Wells provide, or for its insight into the requirements and opportunities federal past performance presents.

Uniquely, this book also provides insights from the federal government's perspective. That side is rarely represented. In fact, this book could be a good tutorial for federal officials hoping to quickly come up to speed on the requirements and burdens imposed on them and on their contractors. That knowledge will help make government officials smarter commentators on contractors' past performance and more sophisticated consumers of contractor past performance reports.

Don't expect to find a simple checklist for success here, because the authors' thoughtful commentary and insights permeate this book. But those readers who are committed to success in the increasingly challenging federal market will find tools and actionable strategies they can put into practice immediately. The message is clear: Don't wait to get started on the journey to "winning with past performance."

—Alan Chvotkin
Executive Vice President and Counsel
Professional Services Council[1]

---

[1] The Professional Services Council is the leading national trade association of firms providing professional and technology services to the federal government. The views expressed here are Alan Chvotkin's own and do not necessarily represent the views of the Professional Services Council or any of its members.

PREFACE

This book is about past performance. It seeks to provide a well-rounded perspective that includes both industry and government points of view. As such, we intend it to inform, advise, and challenge those of us doing business with the government as well as those doing business for the government. We hope it will help aspiring government contractors, government procurement officials, and program managers improve company and contractor performance as well as the management and use of past performance information on both sides of the contracting process. We all share the same goal—to bring awareness of the significance of firm past performance and get it to speak volumes about a particular bidder's ability to deliver the best results—cost-effectively and at the lowest risk to the government.

In spite of almost two decades of spotlight focus by the federal government on past performance as a means to distinguish among bidders, both the collection and use of past performance information remain disjointed, siloed, and not well understood by either government or industry. There has been practically zero literature of any significance published on the subject that is geared toward helping contractors, whose livelihoods depend on how their past performance information is collected and used by the government. Additionally, there is little in the literature that presents balanced government and industry viewpoints on the subject. Finally, there is no voice in the conversation that succinctly presents the universe of uses and issues associated with past performance. The few texts available essentially take the construct of the current past performance information system as a given and provide little analysis, evaluation, or examination of this system.

Our goal with this book is to fully examine past performance as a business tool, to increase awareness, improve understanding, and promote the adoption and use of smart business practices on both the buyer and seller sides of the past performance equation. Our decades of experience in both industry and government have included dealing with every aspect of firm past performance, ranging from deciding when and how to collect past performance information to evaluating responses to past performance questionnaires, assembling industry teams based on past performance, crafting hundreds of proposals and navigating contractor performance assessment report completion with government clients.

Our intent is to convey three overarching themes:

1. Well-informed buyers and sellers seek to understand what their counterparts on the other side of the buy/sell process go through. Hence, informed buyers and sellers temper their actions and activities based on this knowledge. They gather as much knowledge as possible about the impact of their actions on the other party, on the acquisition, and on the outcomes sought.

2. The highest and best use of past performance information and other customer satisfaction inputs is to impact execution and, therefore, actually improve performance and operations.

3. Both buyers and sellers want to know each other's identity. They both want to know and understand the other. *Who organizations are* is perpetuated and understood through stories. Past performance information reported by the buyer and past performance write-ups included by the seller with proposals *are* these stories and have common features and scripts.

Readers of this book will find immediately useful tools for assessing a firm's past performance, for implementing active management of past performance information in both government agencies and private firms, and for facilitating discussion. Readers will also benefit from a holistic look at past performance from all angles and perspectives. This book "brings it all together" on the subject of past performance and is a ready reference source for buyers, sellers, policymakers, contracting professionals, service providers, and others.

This book is intended to be read from beginning to end. However, a complete index and detailed table of contents are provided, and much material is provided in a manner such that sections or specific exhibits can be pulled out for direct use or reference. The discussion is presented in eight chapters, starting with the context of past performance. Exhibits are included after several chapters to provide additional content, examples, and other supporting materials. Acronyms used are provided along with definitions used in the book and a complete index.

Understanding the core components of past performance and how past performance information is used is essential for agencies, contractors, and bidders. It is frequently a central element of the evaluation process used by nearly all government agencies when they determine which proposals will be awarded contracts. Chapter 1 defines *past performance* and discusses the history of the use of past performance by the U.S. government. It provides an overview of the collection, evaluation, and use of past performance information.

Mastery of the buyer's process for obtaining, evaluating, and using past performance information is especially critical for sellers as they seek to showcase themselves in all potential repositories the buyer might turn to for information about their past performance. Choices made during the collection and evaluation of past performance information are critical to contract award decisions. Chapter 2 is in some ways the heart of the book and presents the cycle of past performance from both the buyer's and the seller's perspectives. For the buyer, the cycle includes evaluation, storage/retention, and use. For the seller, the cycle includes collection, interpretation, storage/retention, and use.

Contractors need to adopt a methodical approach to the past performance write-up section of their proposals that helps them develop a compelling story about their experience and qualifications to perform at a high level for a project on which they plan to bid. Chapter 3 approaches the presentation of past performance as a form of storytelling and takes the reader through four levels of presenting past performance information: giving just the facts, providing context, providing impact, and increasing understanding. Sample write-ups are included for each level.

As should be clear, Chapter 3 is primarily for sellers or presenters of past performance write-ups in proposals. What is not so obvious is that it is also written for buyers: Truly *informed* buyers understand what their counterparts on the other side of the buy/sell go through. In situations such as those found in the government contracting market, where the buyer dictates the form and content of the information it receives, it is not always easy as a buyer to completely understand and foresee the implications of decisions and instructions.

Obtaining maximum value from past performance information repositories requires developing, implementing, and executing policies, procedures, architectures, and technologies that take security, the user experience, data as an asset, and openness into consideration. Chapter 4 is about what past performance information gets stored, who stores it, how they store it, how it is accessed, and how it is managed in the aggregate. Three categories of repositories are discussed: government repositories, privately maintained repositories containing information about multiple sellers that provide fee-based access, and repositories maintained by a firm for use by the firm.

Past performance information is evaluated by the government as part of responsibility determinations, as part of source selection evaluations, and as a part of monitoring contractor performance. Although the focus here is on the federal government as the evaluator of a firm's past performance, evaluations also impact how a company will be considered when evaluated by potential business partners, financial institutions, employees, and investors as they make decisions, including contract award decisions. Chapter 5 provides a detailed discussion of buyer evaluations of performance in responsibility determinations, as a part of monitoring contractor performance, and during source selection.

Chapter 5 also presents a unique and comprehensive past performance ranking tool that can be pulled out and put to immediate use in a firm or used to guide a discussion in a government office. The chapter provides the complete, as issued, past performance instructions to offerors and an evaluation scheme issued by a government agency and used to conduct a procurement in 2013. A critique of this solicitation segment highlights the impact on both the buyer and the seller from the use of this scheme.

A strong grasp of how the government views disputes and protests over past performance issues is critical for any firm that pursues a challenge to a contract decision based on its past performance. Chapter 6 discusses venues, the timing of disputes, and basis of appeals. Three case studies redacted from Government Accountability Office (GAO) decisions are provided. Discussion questions are provided with the cases as well as possible answers to the discussion questions. These cases have been used a number of times in courses taught by the authors and have proven to be an effective tool to generate meaningful classroom interaction and learning experiences.

The collection and use of past performance information by the government continue to be refined and improved. Success with past performance requires staying abreast of these changes and understanding their causes and directions. Chapter 7 illuminates the changing face of past performance: During the time this book was written, there has been much focus, attention, and action on past performance regulation, policy, and use by the government. The Introduction looked back to the origination of the use of past performance by the government as a buyer and its early history. Chapter 7 picks up this thread and discusses how and why the use of past performance is changing. Also included in this chapter is an examination of what can be learned from interest groups, industry associations, commercial buyers, and others.

Widespread adoption of seller performance feedback measures as an important element of sales transactions is occurring across many industries and markets. The expectations established with buyers and sellers based on this adoption will affect the collection, evaluation, and use of past performance information in the government contracting market. Chapter 8 examines how the use of past performance may look in the future by discussing ten trends most likely to be witnessed in the relatively near future.

—*Jim Hiles*
Jim@winningwithpastperformance.com

—*Earl Wells*
Earl@winningwithpastperformance.com

ACKNOWLEDGMENTS

We started on the journey of this book thinking it would be a much shorter trip than it turned out to be. It has also been even more rewarding, educational, and inspiring than we had imagined.

A special note of thanks for her forbearance and her encouragement goes to Myra Strauss, our editorial and spiritual guide. The very generous and timely input and wisdom of Sam Knowles also are greatly appreciated.

Thank you to friends and family who have supported us and participated with us in the journey. Thanks also to our many friends, colleagues, fellow commiserators, and past performance pontificators, who—sometimes knowingly, sometimes not—helped us to refine our thinking and expanded our horizons.

INTRODUCTION

Performance evaluation is not, at base, an arcane concept. We all use performance evaluations in some capacity to guide our purchase decisions, whether we are buying items off the shelf at an established retail outlet or hiring a local carpenter to install cabinets in our kitchens. Indeed, we use past performance information *even if there isn't any,* because the absence of any knowledge of past performance informs how we think about or judge a prospective seller, and this informs our thinking on the seller's future performance. When we buy something important, do we want to buy it from someone who will be "learning on the job" on *our* job? Or do we want to buy that item or service from someone who has provided it previously, perhaps to other buyers?

The same holds true for the government when it is determining which aspiring offeror should be awarded a project. Over time, the federal government has evolved the following process for choosing the best performer for a job: Government representatives assemble a solicitation with specific guidelines and parameters that they need the bidder to address—regarding, among other things, the bidder's past performance. After receiving all responses, they evaluate the information and award a contract based in part on the history of the bidder's contract performance.

The question of how to best gather and judge information about past performance has been a challenge for the government from the very beginning. Consider the problem confronting the American colonies at the outset of the Revolutionary War, when creating a navy and acquiring the ships that would make it up was a matter of utmost importance to their defense and security. At the time that the colonies began contracting out for ships to be built, warship design and construction was solely the province of national governments and their shipyards. Since this monopoly was controlled by nations (e.g., Britain) not necessarily disposed to sell to the Americans, the Continental Congress' Naval Committee did not have access to a whole category of shipbuilders. An additional factor for the Congress to consider when hiring contractors to design and build warships (as opposed to fishing vessels) was the recent advance of the use of detailed blueprints from which to build. A buyer making highly consequential ship-purchasing decisions would be wise to consider the varied experience of American shipbuilders and their workforces in following blueprints, as well as with current naval warship construction techniques.

How were they to make decisions about to whom they would award these valuable contracts? At a basic level, if we want to have a ship built, would we hire a person or a company that makes barrels or distills whiskey, or would we naturally turn to a company whose main focus has been building ships? This line of thinking naturally points the buyer toward a focus on past performance: Has this company built ships before? What types of ships? How good or effective were the ships built by this company?

There were several other notable elements of shipbuilding in the 1700s. British naval ship design had stagnated, and this was an active period of shipbuilding in the American colonies. A number of naval ships were built in the colonies, and wars between France, Spain, and England, from the War of the Spanish Succession through the French and Indian War, brought captured warships into colonial ports, where astute shipbuilders could study them. A number of privately owned shipyards that had recently built ships for the British Navy had retained the employees who had worked on these recently ended efforts and had a cadre of workers who had studied captured warships operated in the colonies (Chapelle, 1949).

Therefore, with specific ideas of the types of vessels and the number and placement of guns needed, the Naval Committee turned to the previous experience and performance of prospective shipbuilders and outfitters to base its decisions regarding which American shipbuilder would fulfill these needs. This use of past performance assisted the Naval Committee in discriminating between prospective sellers.

Although past performance is a natural consideration and has been used as an implied evaluation factor, this use was not formalized by the

U.S. government until the 1960s through a Department of Defense past performance reporting system, the Contractor Performance Report.[2] This system was in place for 11 years before DoD concluded that the costs of the program outweighed its benefits and it was discontinued (Edwards, 1995).

Lessons that carry through from this history are reflected in the 1997 National Performance Review benchmarking study report, which noted

> All high-performance organizations whether public or private are, and must be, interested in developing and deploying effective performance measurement and performance management systems, since it is only through such systems that they can remain high-performance organizations.[3]

For sellers, the lessons are to actively manage and understand their current performance as a feedback mechanism to develop better capabilities and higher performance, as well as to understand how, when, and why the government will need to rely on past performance information in buying decisions. For buyers, the lessons are to be aware of the market and market factors that enable meaningful discrimination between prospective suppliers and to recognize and act on the appropriate use of past performance as one of those factors.

Since the founding of the United States, the role of past performance in government evaluations and contract awards has continually produced challenges for contractors and government officials desiring to understand, manage, and work with it.

Today, great strides have been made in ensuring improved and increased access by government officials to pertinent past performance information. These improvements include standardization of the past performance information that is collected, how it is collected, where it is collected, and how and by whom it is accessed. Such advances

---

[2] Described in DoD Directive 5126.38, *Program of Contractor Performance Evaluation*, April 1, 1963, and implemented in Armed Services Procurement Regulation § 1.908 (32 *CFR* § 1.908).

[3] govinfo.library.unt.edu/npr/library/papers/benchmrk/nprbook.html.

have helped alleviate some of the frustrations that contractors and government officials have expressed with cataloging and accessing past performance information. However, there is still a demand for— and considerable room for—improvement. Gaps that remain include consistent completion of past performance reviews, uniformity in documenting past performance, adherence to past performance information collection protocols, accessibility, and the timeliness of past performance information collection.

Chapter 1

PAST PERFORMANCE IN CONTEXT

Past performance is frequently a central element of the process used by nearly all government agencies when they evaluate companies and proposals to determine which ones will be awarded contracts. A company's past performance therefore helps connect it to the government agency acquiring products or services. For this reason, a strong grasp of past performance and its core components is essential to understanding the role it plays in government contracting. The three main elements of past performance are *relevance*, *experience*, and *performance*. The specific differences and similarities between these elements depend on the interpretation and use of past performance information by the government agency.

Most individuals who work for someone else are subject to and familiar with a close analogy to past performance—that of the performance evaluations commonly used to determine pay and pay raises, recommendations for promotion, or otherwise ensure they are an asset to the companies they work for. Performance evaluations are by their nature backward-looking; the evaluation is necessarily of performance that has already occurred; hence the word "past." The use of firm past performance by the government is similar. The government uses past performance as an evaluation factor to determine the fit and positive impact that a specific business entity would have on the project for which it has created a solicitation.

To closely and accurately analyze the history of a firm, we must examine how it has conducted its business in the past and determine whether it has the specific proven expertise that lends strength to its past performance evaluation in context. For example, a shipbuilding entity likely has experience building ships—that is a fairly safe assumption. The key is identifying the business' exact experience that is beneficial to the project it is vying for. Does its experience lie in laying keels or putting up sides? Or does it outfit interiors or install command and control systems? Is its experience in building one rowboat at a time as a jobber to a major shipbuilding company, or is it as a prime contractor managing the design and build-out of a new line of advanced frigates? The experience must be linked to the project the contractor is bidding on. This is the concept of *relevance*.

Many business schools teach a lesson regarding the individual who claims to have 20 years of "experience." Claims such as that are not particularly interesting or noteworthy. After all, it does not tell us anything specific about the person or the experience. People commonly may have been employed in a particular field for the past 20 years. But have they grown their expertise during their career, or become specialists? Some people shy away from opportunities to learn and continue to grow professionally; they essentially have one year of experience 20 times over. It's people who continue to educate themselves, challenge themselves, and make strides to become up-to-date experts in certain areas who can truly claim 20 years of experience. This is the concept of *experience*.

But a firm's raw experience, while important, is not as critical as its performance. Government agencies need to know how well a firm has performed its project responsibilities in the past. The shipbuilder may have built the ship's hull, but it is important to know that the ship stayed afloat, demonstrated maneuverability suitable for naval operations, and achieved other desired results, such as crew survivability or increased time between maintenance. This is the concept of *performance*.

DEFINITION

Our reference to the "system" of collection, retention, and use of past performance information is meant to refer to the overall ecosystem, meaning the aggregate of behaviors, methods, norms, and so on that make up the commonalities of collection, evaluation, retention, and use of past performance information across the government contracting market. The Federal Acquisition Regulation (FAR) has definitions for more than 247 terms that relate to procurement, and in FAR 2.101 defines past performance as *an offeror's or contractor's performance on active and physically completed contracts*. In the FAR, the term *past performance* appears approximately 20 times spelled out and a little more than 100 times abbreviated as *PP*. It is apparent that past performance is a substantial part of the government acquisition process although it is minimally defined, perhaps because it is an all-encompassing concept that involves many details and varying perspectives. Whatever the reason for the simple definition, knowledge and awareness of how past performance is evaluated are critical to successful proposals to perform government work.

One of the most succinct definitions of past performance is that it is an evaluation factor (Edwards, 1995). Past performance defined as an evaluation factor distinguishes it from past performance *information*, or relevant information about a contractor's actions under previously awarded contracts (Edwards, 1995 and 2005). In this volume, however, we will not limit the term *past performance* to an evaluation factor and will use the definition put forth by Edwards in 1995:

> "Past performance" is a composite of three things: (1) observations of the historical facts of a company's work experience—what work it did, when and where it did it, whom it did it for, and what methods it used; (2) qualitative judgments about the breadth, depth and relevance of that experience based on those observations; and (3) qualitative judgments about how well the company performed, also based on those observations. (p. 25)

COLLECTING PAST PERFORMANCE INFORMATION

Government agencies have several methods of collecting past performance information that shows relevant experience and performance. They can review files from prior contracts, evaluate the information submitted by the offeror in a proposal, and reach out to a firm's past customers with direct conversation by e-mail or phone or they may use questionnaires. Other sources and information that the government refers to are law enforcement bureaus, the Better Business Bureau, consumer protection agencies, business credit reports, and other measures of creditworthiness (Edwards, 2005).

It is also important for contractors to know that their past clients are satisfied. If a client hesitates to give thoughtful positive feedback to address concerns, or a mutually acceptable compromise cannot be reached, then consideration should be given to not using that client as a past performance reference.

If an offeror becomes aware of the potential that a specific client may provide negative feedback if queried about the firm's past performance, it typically has time to respond and should do so. The evaluating government agency that first discovers or becomes aware of negative past performance information has the responsibility to inform the firm of the adverse information and allow them an opportunity to respond, rectify, or provide supporting documentation that presents its perspective on the information (FAR 15.306).

An unintended result of the increased use of past performance and associated queries to government personnel, such as past performance questionnaires (PPQs) and contractor performance assessment reports (CPARs), is PPQ/CPAR fatigue. Government clients of frequently bidding firms become annoyed or burdened by the associated "hurry up and submit them" PPQ requests. This fatigue is evident in some agencies' decisions to not provide PPQs or participate in other forms of customer satisfaction surveys and measurements.

EVALUATING PAST PERFORMANCE

As stated, three main criteria make up the standards for evaluating past performance (Nash et al., 1998):

- Observation of a company's historical facts
- Qualitative judgments about the breadth, depth, and relevance of projects

- Qualitative judgments regarding how a company performed based on observations.

These three criteria allow the government to get the full scope of a bidder's ability to do a similar project in the present or future.

Organizations should develop a portfolio of past performance projects that gives them relevant experience for the types of contracts that they wish to bid on. The government evaluates a contractor's actions under previously awarded contracts, including its ability to meet contract specifications, provide good workmanship, control costs, keep to a schedule, cooperate and otherwise exhibit reasonable behavior, achieve high customer satisfaction, and demonstrate concern for customer well-being (FAR 42.1501).

We mentioned earlier that *experience* and *past performance* are often used interchangeably. This holds true in the FAR. However, some government agencies show differences between the two. Although the FAR does not specifically define *experience*, agencies define it as *the kind and amount of work that an offeror has done*. This definition distinguishes experience from past performance as *an assessment of how well an offeror did in past work*, and it is the meaning used in this book.

One of the best things about experience from an organizational or government point of view is that it presents opportunity to learn from errors, improve systems, and grow. This inevitably improves an organization's relevant experience because it will develop a history of problem-solving—or, better yet, problem *prevention*.

Relevant Experience as It Relates to Past Performance

Depending on the specific circumstances under which past performance is being evaluated, in addition to the past performance and experience of the firm, the past performance and experience of key personnel, subcontractors, predecessor companies, and project managers may be cited in a proposal. Including individuals or organizations in a proposal that are *not* proposed as an active part of the project being bid is less relevant than referencing individuals and organizations that *are* proposed. The focus must remain on highlighting the relevant experience within the abilities of the individuals or organizations that will be involved with the project the firm is bidding on. This is reaffirmed by FAR 15.305, which states that evaluations should take into account past performance information regarding predecessor companies, key personnel with relevant experience, or subcontractors that will perform major or critical aspects of the solicitation requirements of the project being bid on, when such information is relevant to the acquisition.

There are two opposing, complementary approaches an evaluation scheme can take to relevant experience for past performance purposes. These approaches can be blended in a variety of ways. One is to accept the performance of an offeror's project managers, key personnel, and subcontractors as past performance for that offeror. The other option is to evaluate the offeror on its own record and specifically exclude the performance of its project managers, key personnel, and subcontractors. The first option can obscure the fact that an offeror may have no relevant experience *as a company* for this specific bid. This is especially true if it hires people who have relevant experience just for the project and purposes of submitting the proposal (Edwards, 2005).

Firms new to the government contracting market, of course, must have a starting point, which may appear to an evaluator as a lack of relevant experience. FAR 15.305 states a "neutral rule" that in cases where an offeror has no relevant past performance experience or for whom information on past performance is not available, that offeror may not be evaluated—favorably *or* unfavorably—on past performance. The spirit and intent of this rule is that a firm with *no* record of performance is different from a firm with a record of *poor* performance. To maintain this spirit, the comment "none" or "no record" will usually be incorporated into the review when there is no relevant experience. The information is neither good nor bad: One cannot give a negative review of something that does not exist.

Although the government may not downgrade a contractor for lack of relevant experience under the neutral rule, that does not mean that contractors without relevant experience will be rated as favorably as an offeror that has sound relevant experience. This is important to keep in mind, and a bidder must include details and emphasis in other sections of the proposal to give strength and merit to the offeror's proposal when the offeror has no relevant past performance.

Relevant is loosely defined by the government. Most offerors should be able to find some past experiences to place in the relevant experience area. It may seem a reach at times, but if it shows initiative, determination, and successful results, it will speak positively about the aspirations and potential of the contractor. If done correctly (see Chapter 5), this is more favorable than "none" or "no record."

Use of Past Performance as an Evaluation Factor

Both buyers (agencies) and sellers (bidders/offerors) evaluate past performance and have much at stake when doing so. However, the government is working to award a contract and the bidder is working to get the best rating and receive the award. The purpose of past performance as an evaluation factor is to help the government distinguish between offerors who are vying for government contracts. Bidders, on the other hand, are evaluating their own performances to select those projects that maximize their past performance evaluations.

The most effective way for a firm to relate or share past performance experiences is through telling a story. Thinking of the presentation of past performance information as a story helps to lay out the scenario, show the solutions that were developed and used, detail any obstacles and how they were overcome, and demonstrate the outcome and impact of the firm's efforts on the agency's mission.

Use of Past Performance by the Buyer

Past performance evaluations are used by the buyer to assess the risk of award to a specific offeror—the "risk" of satisfactory performance if an award is made to that specific offeror. When considering an offeror's record of past performance, government agencies can and may evaluate the past performance information gleaned from an offeror's proposal along with information from other sources, such as the evaluating agency's direct knowledge, government repositories (e.g., the Past Performance Information Retrieval System), or direct conversation with/questionnaires from other government agencies. However, the relevant experience that a contractor relates through the past performance stories in its proposal, in most cases, will be the primary and in many cases the only source of past performance information used by the evaluating agency to determine the qualifications and value of the contractor.

The information that the government is looking for will be specified in the solicitation. Straying from what is requested will not usually result in a favorable outcome for the offeror. For example, as an offeror, you may have a completed project that went phenomenally well—it may even be your crown jewel. But if that experience does not relate to the upcoming project, it will not help obtain a more favorable rating from the government agency.

The stories that an offeror tells are evaluated, analyzed, confirmed, and weighted by the government evaluation team or evaluator. The specific approach used to perform this evaluation is dependent on numerous factors, including the size and scope of the procurement, the level of competition expected or achieved, and the availability of government personnel to perform the evaluation. Government personnel have varying degrees of knowledge, experience, and skills in conducting these evaluations. Their ability to dissect the pertinent past performance information submitted and discern the important and relevant elements is at the heart of the evaluation. That is why a well-told story, based on fact, is so important for a firm that wishes to succeed in the competitive government contracting market.

Use of Past Performance by the Seller

Stories and other elements of past performance information that a contractor shares in its bid for government work should express the unique pieces of information that help it stand apart from other offerors. Reporting a success with "We did teamwork, found solutions to unexpected problems, and reached a satisfactory conclusion" is not a unique story. Organizations need to provide specific details and to elaborate how the conclusion would have been different had anybody else been involved. These details create the distinction between a firm's experiences being truly unique and the firm's merely *hoping* they are unique.

When an organization is attempting to sell its goods or services to a government agency, it must use its past performance to show the relevance of the work it has done previously and carry it to the present. However, government agencies typically limit the inclusion of past performance information in proposals to a time period, such as the previous three or five years.

Stories persistently retold in organizations, such as those presented in proposals submitted to government agencies, maintain an organization's identity. These stories are either influenced by the organization or they are not. There is a saying about social media: The question is not *whether* you have a social media presence. You do—you just might not have created it yourself. Past performance is a similar phenomenon. Sellers cannot dictate their identities to a buyer, at least not as much as they would like to. Some stories about firms are told by others, as in Contractor Performance Assessment Reporting System (CPARS) reports for example. Sellers do describe their past performance and explain "who they are" to the best of their ability, and many times these descriptions are tailored to very specific audiences of buyers. Buyers rely upon stories from multiple sources to determine the seller's identity and to understand the seller's identity in the specific context of a bid or purchasing decision.

Because people are attracted to organizations with persistent stories that end in positive outcomes, contractors must create factually accurate stories that show how their abilities and efforts led to the desired results for their customers. In the same way, evaluators are attracted to stories of past performance that are easily relatable to their current requirements and challenges—*and* that make it very clear the contractor not only has achieved positive outcomes in the past but can achieve them in the future. The most common organizational story has the following script: organizational members confront a problem, the employees take action, and the problem is either solved or not. Past performance guidance in solicitations, without using this language, frequently asks for these elements in proposals.

Whatever script is followed, the stories a contractor tells about its past performance will be viewed as either favorable or unfavorable by the evaluator. The aspiring bidder needs to find ways to make the story both unique *and* relevant to the evaluating audience by detailing *specific* actions taken to reach a favorable outcome for past customers.

PROBLEMS WITH PAST PERFORMANCE

The Government Accountability Office (GAO) noted in 2009 that "contracting officials" agreed that for past performance information to be useful for sharing, it must be documented, relevant, and reliable. However, GAO's review of the Past Performance Information Retrieval System (PPIRS) data for fiscal years 2006 and 2007 indicates that only a small percentage of contracts had a documented performance assessment and that reluctance to rely more on past performance was due in part to skepticism about the reliability of the information and difficulty assessing relevance to specific acquisitions (GAO, 2009).

HISTORY OF GOVERNMENT USE

Use of past performance is not a new concept in the government's buying decisions; however, the "mandatory" use of past performance as a source selection evaluation factor is a recent phenomenon, as is the collection and centralization of past performance information (Nash et al., 1998). Nevertheless, the government has increasingly relied on past performance in source selection decisions. As a result, increasing the collection, evaluation, documentation, and utility derived from past performance information as an evaluation factor (and in the adjudication of contractor performance incentives, as discussed in Chapter 5) has been the subject not only of numerous acquisition regulations and policies but also of repeated reform efforts and highly critical government watchdog reports.

The first notable attempt to formalize the use of past performance information in government procurements occurred in the early 1960s. This was precipitated in part by growing pressure to achieve more competition in procurements, following a period marked by heavy use of sealed bidding procedures that had the effect of limiting bid evaluations to price and technical compliance. During that decade, procurement methods that included the adoption of contractor performance evaluation programs were created (Whelan, 1992). For example, the Department of Defense (DoD) implemented a departmentwide past performance evaluation system in 1963 that was subsequently abandoned in 1971 after a conclusion that the benefits of the system did not outweigh the costs.[4]

Since then, several significant legislative and regulatory developments prescribing the use of past performance information have led to the concept of past performance as it is understood and used today. (Exhibit 1-A, at the end of this chapter, provides a more detailed timeline of events and regulations of significance in the history of past performance use by the government.)

Competition in Contracting Act (1984)

In 1984, the Competition in Contracting Act was passed to ensure increased competition for government contracts, which was to result in reduced costs of purchased goods and services. The act formally defined a "responsible source" of services and supplies. Among other attributes, a responsible source or contractor has a satisfactory performance record and a satisfactory record of business ethics.

Brooks Act (1992)

The Brooks Act amended the Federal Property and Administrative Services Act of 1949 to address what had been viewed as a propensity to award contracts to the lowest-priced bidder without paying adequate attention to the qualifications of the awardee to design and manage projects with significant public safety elements, such as bridges and highways.

---

[4] Revision 10 to Armed Services Procurement Regulations, Nov. 30, 1971.

This act established a procurement process to select architect and engineering firms for award of design contracts by the government, codifying a qualifications-based selection process. This process focused on the negotiation of contracts following a firm's selection based on demonstrated competence and professional qualification for the services required. Under this qualifications-based process, price quotes are not initially considered.

If the agency is unable to negotiate a satisfactory contract with the firm considered to be the most qualified, at a price determined by the government to be fair and reasonable, negotiations with that firm end and new negotiations are begun with the second most qualified firm, and so on until a contract is awarded. This process is still followed today and is an exemplar for the use of past performance information as a primary source selection evaluation factor.

Federal Acquisition Streamlining Act (1994)

The Federal Acquisition Streamlining Act amended provisions enacted by the Competition in Contracting Act and other federal procurement law. Its purpose was to simplify the federal procurement process by reducing paperwork burdens, facilitating the acquisition of commercial items, enhancing the use of simplified procedures for small purchases, increasing the use of electronic commerce, and otherwise improving procurement process efficiency.

The act established a governmentwide requirement to formally document contractor past performance and to use past performance information to evaluate sources, make source selection decisions, and make responsibility determinations. The original threshold for this mandate was that all agencies must evaluate every prime contractor's performance on contracts in excess of $1 million. This threshold was decreased to $100,000 in January 1998.

Clinger-Cohen Act (1996)

The Clinger-Cohen Act established a comprehensive approach for executive agencies to improve the acquisition and management of their information resources. This act established the chief information officer position at agencies and created a program to use solutions-based contracting for acquisitions of information technology that relied upon source selection factors emphasizing the qualifications of the offeror. These offeror qualifications included as factors personnel skills, previous experience in providing other private or public sector organizations with solutions for attaining objectives similar to the objectives of the acquisition, past contract performance, qualifications of the proposed program manager, and the proposed management plan. Although the act did not specifically call out "relevance," it did emphasize considering a broader range of past performance experiences that could be considered relevant, such as commercial work performed and the experience of key persons.

Elements of the Brooks Act were repealed by the Clinger-Cohen Act, but the use of qualifications-based selection continues and is included in FAR part 36.

Office for Federal Procurement Policy Guide (2000)

The Office for Federal Procurement Policy (OFPP) has the authority to prescribe guidance for executive agencies regarding standards for evaluating the past performance of contractors and collecting and maintaining information on past contract performance. In 2000, OFPP published discretionary guidance in a best practices guide available online.[5]

In the guide *(Best Practices for Collecting and Using Current and Past Performance Information)*, OFPP states that agencies are required to assess contractor performance after a contract is completed and that they must maintain and share performance records with other agencies. The guidance encourages agencies to make contractor performance records an essential consideration in the award of negotiated acquisitions, and it gives guidelines for evaluation.

OFPP noted the importance of distinguishing comparative past performance evaluations used in an evaluation trade-off process from pass/fail performance evaluations. It goes on to point out that a

---

[5] www.whitehouse.gov/omb/best_practice_re_past_perf.

comparative past performance evaluation conducted using a tradeoff process seeks to identify the degree of risk associated with each competing offeror, i.e., that the evaluation describes the degree of confidence the government has in the offeror's likelihood of success.

The guide also encourages agencies to establish automated mechanisms to record and disseminate performance information. Performance records should specifically address performance in the areas of cost, schedule, technical performance (quality of product or service), and business relations, including customer satisfaction, using a five-point adjectival rating scale (i.e., Exceptional, Very Good, Satisfactory, Marginal, and Unsatisfactory; OFPP, 2000).

Contractor Performance Assessment Reporting System (2004)

CPARS originated in 1996 and has been designated as the DoD's solution for collecting contractor performance information since 2004. CPARS has since evolved into the government enterprise solution for collection and retention of contractor past performance information. The titling of the program, program elements, and references in user guides and reports in the system were revised to remove DoD specifics in 2011. *CPARS* refers to this system in its entirety. The main activity associated with this system is the documentation of contractor and grantee performance information that is required by federal regulations. This is accomplished in web-enabled reports referred to as *CPARS reports*. CPARS currently contains three modules:

1. CPARS for performance assessments on systems, services, IT, and operations support contracts

2. Architect-Engineer Contract Administration Support System (ACASS) for performance assessments on architect-engineer contracts

3. Construction Contractor Appraisal Support System (CCASS) for performance assessments on construction contracts.

Department of Defense Inspector General Report (2008)

The efficiency and accuracy of government contract awards being reported to CPARS was reviewed by the DoD inspector general in 2008 (in *Contractor Past Performance Information*). It found that government acquisition officials do not have all the past performance information needed to make informed decisions related to market research, contract awards, and other acquisition matters. It also noted that CPARS did not contain information on all active system contracts over $5 million. Of the reports that should have been in CPARS, 39 percent were registered more than a year late, 68 percent had performance reports that were overdue, and 82 percent did not contain detailed, sufficient narratives to establish that the past performance ratings they contained were credible and justifiable.

In response to this report, one of the actions being taken by DoD is to remove any records in the system for contractor performance that began in 2007 or earlier for which no action other than contract data entry has occurred.

Duncan Hunter National Defense Authorization Act (2008)

This bill was first introduced in 2008 by Senator Carl Levin of Michigan and became law on October 14, 2008. Its purpose was to authorize appropriations for the fiscal year 2009 for all DoD military activities. This act emphasized the use of past performance information systems and the use of past performance in source selections by requiring the Administrator of General Services (Office of Management and Budget) to establish and maintain a database of information regarding the integrity and performance of grant and contract awardees of federal agency contracts and grants above the threshold of $500,000 for use by contracting officials.

The act also requires agency officials responsible for contract or grant awards to review the database of past performance information and to consider other past performance information available with respect to the offeror in making any responsibility determination or past performance evaluation for such offeror. The act also requires documenting in contract files the "manner in which the material in past performance databases was considered" in any responsibility determination or past performance evaluation.

Contractor Performance Assessment Rating System Policy (2011)

The CPARS policy and guidebook underwent significant revisions between 2011 and 2014 to reflect changes in the evolving user base, changes to the FAR, and changes in the way the system is used. This policy document and guide states that the contractor performance evaluations contained in CPARs are a method of recording contractor performance and should not be the sole method for reporting on it to the contractor. Government policy is that CPARs should be an objective report of contractor performance during a period against contract requirements. Completing CPARs is the responsibility of the designated assessing official, who may be a program manager or the equivalent individual responsible for program, project, or task/job/delivery/order execution. It may also mean the performance evaluator, quality assurance evaluator, requirements indicator, or contracting officer's representative. CPARS information is passed to the PPIRS.

FAR 42.15 Revision (2013)

FAR 42.15, on contractor performance information, was revised in September 2013 to detail and standardize the when, where, who, what, and how of contractor performance evaluation and documentation. Existing contractor appeals processes were left in place. The revision made clarifying language changes along with these four significant revisions:

- 42.1502 states that past performance evaluations for contracts and orders should be prepared at least annually and when the work under the contract or order is completed.
- 42.1503(b) adds a new requirement that past performance reports must include a clear, nontechnical description of the

principal purpose of the contract or order and standardizes past performance evaluation factors. The subpart also includes a minimum set of evaluation factors and a standardized rating scale. The minimum factors include:

o   Technical (quality of product or service)

o   Cost control (not applicable to firm fixed-price contracts)

o   Schedule/timeliness

o   Management or business relations

o   Small business subcontracting (as applicable)

o   Other (as applicable).

The ratings are:

o   Exceptional

o   Very Good

o   Satisfactory

o   Marginal

o   Unsatisfactory.

- 42.1503(c) adds a new requirement that agencies enter any award-fee performance adjectival rating and incentive-fee contract performance evaluations into CPARS.

- 42.1503(e) adds a new requirement that agencies conduct frequent evaluations of agency compliance with past performance evaluation requirements.

Although the collection of past performance information is currently required and specified in FAR 42.1502, an important distinction to note is that there is discretion regarding whether past performance has to be used as a source selection factor.[6]

Much energy and effort has been applied toward improving the collection and retention of and access to contractor past performance information by the government, in particular by DoD. Progress is slow, and by most accounts neither long-term goals (standardize

_____

[6] FAR 15.304(c)(3).

contracting ratings used by agencies, provide more meaningful past performance information, develop a centralized questionnaire system for sharing government wide, eliminate multiple systems that feed performance information into PPIRS) nor short-term goals (revising the FAR to mandate the use of PPIRS) for past performance information management have been achieved in a timely fashion, if at all. This can be attributed to an underestimation by government agencies of the challenges involved.

Exhibit 1-A: Past Performance History Timeline

Year	Source/Report No.	Item	Impact
1962	Report to the President on Government Contracting, April 30, 1962	Bell Committee (a Blue Ribbon committee) is appointed by President Kennedy	Presidential-level recommendations that included exchanges of information between agencies regarding contractor evaluations.
1962	P. Kayafas. *Contractor Past Performance: Basis for Contract Award.* Professional Study No. 3940 at 23 (Maxwell AFB, Ala.: Air War College, April 1970)	President directs that the recommendations of the Bell Committee be implemented	An elaborate Contractor Performance Evaluation (CPE) system was devised to document and disseminate performance data on large-dollar-value contracts.
1963	Described in DoD Directive 5126.38, Program of Contractor Performance Evaluation, April 1, 1963, and implemented in Armed Services Procurement Regulation § 1.908 (32 CFR § 1.908)	DoD implements Past Performance Information (PPI) collection system	First notable attempt to capture PPI in a systematic manner.
1971	Revision 10 to ASPR, Nov. 30, 1971	DoD abandons PPI collection system	Lesson learned on cost vs. benefit regarding PPI collection and archiving: not worth the effort.
1978	AFSC Project STAR, Past Performance Panel Final Report (Oct. 1987)	Air Force Systems Command initiative to use past performance as a source selection consideration	Significant test of the ability and effectiveness of evaluating past performance in source selections. The test showed that a methodology was needed to verify furnished data, not penalize contractors without performance records, and determine relevancy of data to a particular source selection.

Year	Source/Report No.	Item	Impact
1981	Reinhard, M.J., "Improving the Source Selection Process." *Concepts*, Summer 1982, Volume 5, Number 3	Deputy Secretary of Defense Carlucci's "Carlucci Initiatives" consisting of 32 defense acquisition reforms	Noted that logic and common sense dictated using past performance as an evaluation criterion in source selections. Based on previous failed DoD efforts, only encouraged source selection teams to consider past performance in source selections and did not seek to establish a formal contractor performance measurement system.
1984	The Competition in Contracting Act of 1984 (CICA), 41 U.S.C. § 253	Competition in Contracting Act (CICA)	Advocated the use of past performance in government source selections.
1986	Packard Commission Report	Recommends that DoD make greater use of commercial practices, including maintaining a list of qualified suppliers that have held high standards of product quality and reliability	Reinforced government use of commercial best practices that included systematic use of PPI.
1986	10 U.S.C. § 2305	CICA amended and implemented in FAR 15.605(b)	Required quality to be evaluated in every source selection. Quality to be evaluated in part based on prior experience and past performance.
1987	AFSC Project STAR, Past Performance Panel Final Report (Oct. 1987)	Air Force Project STAR study	Concluded that PPI was ineffective because it was inconsistent and thus unreliable. However, the panel found that although the estimated impact of past performance on source selection was nonexistent to slight in most cases, and rarely was the deciding factor, when past performance was a factor, good past performance had a positive impact on the source selection in the majority of cases.

Year	Source/Report No.	Item	Impact
1988	Air Force Systems Command Regulation 800.54, Contractor Performance Assessment	Air Force pilots Contractor Performance Assessment Reporting System for major system acquisition contractors	Lesson learned on scalability of PPI collection and use for major system acquisitions: resource intensive and not scalable.
1989	SECNAV Instruction 4855.7, Department of the Navy Contractor Evaluation System	Navy pilots Red-Yellow-Green contractor performance rating system for field-level contracting	Lesson learned on scalability of PPI collection and use: Subjective past performance evaluations needed for more complex procurements.
1989	Secretary of Defense, Defense Management Report to the President, July 1989	Secretary of Defense Dick Cheney charters joint OSD-DoD task force to expand the CPARS concept DoD-wide	Concluded that a DoD-wide PPI system was not feasible.
1993	OFPP Policy Letter 92-5, Past Performance Information, 58 *Fed. Reg.* 3573 (Jan. 11, 1993)	OFPP issues past performance policy guidance	Required that past performance be a mandatory evaluation factor in competitive negotiations, be considered in responsibility determinations and required that executive agencies collect and use PPI.
1994	Laurent, Anne. "All Eyes on Acquisition Reform," *Government Executive:* 23–25 (August 1997); Ichniowski, Tom. "OMB Test Weighs Past Work," *ENR* 232: 11 (February 1994)	OFPP pilot program to use PPI in source selections	Study showed that on 30 contracts re-competed using PPI, the average customer satisfaction level increased 21 percent over the previous contract.

Year	Source/Report No.	Item	Impact
1994	Public Law No. 103-355 (Oct. 13, 1994)	Federal Acquisition Streamlining Act (FASA)	Two legislative findings: (1) past contract performance is one of the relevant factors that a contracting officer of an executive agency should consider in awarding a contract; (2) it is appropriate for a contracting officer to consider past performance of an offeror as an indicator of its likely future performance. Also established the "neutral rule" wherein firms lacking relevant performance history will receive a neutral evaluation for past performance.
1995	*A Guide to Best Practices for Past Performance, Interim Edition*, May 1995. http://www.acquisition. gov/comp/AcqNet_Library/ OFPP/BestPractices/ BestPract.html	Office of Federal Procurement Policy (OFPP) issues interim *Best Practices for Past Performance* guidebook	OFPP noted that (1) comparative evaluation of past performance is a better method for making "best value" selection decisions than determining the lowest price, and (2) that current evaluation practices "allow offerors that can write outstanding proposals, but may not perform accordingly, to continue to 'win' contracts when other competing offerors have significantly better performance records, and therefore, offer a higher probability of meeting the contract requirements."

Year	Source/Report No.	Item	Impact
1995	*Federal Register*, Vol. 60, No. 62. http://www.gpo.gov/ fdsys/pkg/FR-1995-03-31/ pdf/95-7827.pdf	Federal Acquisition Circular 93-02 as implemented in FAR 15.605	Required that past performance be used as an evaluation factor in all negotiated acquisitions exceeding $1 million not later than July 1, 1995, in all solicitations exceeding $500,000 not later than July 1, 1997, and in all solicitations exceeding $100,000 not later than January 1, 1999.
1996	Little, Arthur D., Inc. "Contractor Evaluation Program: Final Report for the Contractor Past Performance Systems Evaluation Study to the Deputy Under Secretary of Defense (Acquisition Reform)." Contract DAWS01-95-F-2182, 17 June 1996.	Firm Arthur D. Little, Inc., performs study on DoD PP systems	Developed a benchmark of "qualities of an effective PPI system": (1) Implements decentralized approach with general guidelines (2) Focuses on similar product areas or services (3) Views total program context (4) Historically integrated through business area alliances (5) Users help define what gets collected and when (6) Easy to understand and explain (7) Information shared among organizations
1997	*Federal Register*, Vol. 62, No. 189 http://www.gpo.gov/ fdsys/pkg/FR-1997-09-30/ pdf/97-25666.pdf	Federal Acquisition Circular 97-02 and FAR Case 95-209 as implemented in FAR 15.306	Established requirement that offerors shall be granted the opportunity to explain situations that contributed to an adverse past performance rating to which they have not had a previous opportunity to respond before such ratings can be the determining factor for exclusion from the competitive range.

Year	Source/Report No.	Item	Impact
1997	Under Secretary of Defense for Acquisition, Technology and Logistics. 2013. memorandum: *Should Cost Management in Defense Acquisition.* http://www.acq.osd.mil/docs/USA003343-13%20 signed%20memo.pdf	Office of the Under Secretary of Defense for Acquisition, Technology, and Logistics (OSD AT&L) memorandum *Should Cost Management in Defense Acquisition*	Emphasized importance of collecting PPI.
1998	Department of Defense Office of Inspector General. "Contractor Past Performance Information. "Report No. D-2008-057, February 29, 2008. http://www.dodig.mil/Audit/reports/fy08/08-057.pdf	Navy develops Contractor Performance Assessment Reports System (CPARS)	Established enduring system for collecting and archiving PPI.
1998	"DoD Sets Contractor Standards," *Government Executive*, 30: 10 (February 1998)	DoD establishes five-level past performance rating system for almost all categories and sectors of contracts	First large-scale atempt to standardize the collection of PPI.
1999	DoD Class Deviation 99-O0002. https://acc.dau.mil/adl/en-US/341818/file/48034/%23102928%20 Class%20Deviation%20 99-O0002,%20Past%20 Performance.pdf	DoD class waiver increases the minimum thresholds for PP reporting	DoD minimum thresholds for PP reporting increased to $5.5 million for systems and operations support, $1 million for services/information technology, and $100,000 for fuels or health care. These class deviations have been consistently renewed and remain in place in 2014.
2000	Office of Federal Procurement Policy. 2000. Best Practices for Collecting and Using Current and Past Performance Information. http://www.whitehouse.gov/omb/best_practice_re_past_perf.	OFPP issues *Best Practices for Collecting and Using Current and Past Performance Information* guidebook	Emphasizes the importance of fair past performance reporting, frequent two-way communications between government and contractors, clearly documented problem areas, and "no surprises."

Year	Source/Report No.	Item	Impact
2001	Department of the Air Force, Office of the Assistant Secretary, Contracting Policy Memo 01-C-05, Memorandum for ALMAJCOM-FOA-DRU (Contracting) Interim Revision of AFFARS 5342.1501, Contractor Performance Assessment Reporting System (CPARS). http://farsite.hill.af.mil/reghtml/changes/afcpm/01-c-05.htm	Air Force adopts Navy CPARS.	Movement toward CPARS as single collection system for all agencies.
2002	The Office of Management and Budget (OMB) July 3, 2002, memorandum to all Federal agencies. http://www.secnav.navy.mil/rda/OneSource/Pages/eBusiness/DON%20eBusiness%20Solutions/PPIRS.aspx	Past Performance Information Retrieval System (PPIRS) created by the Naval Sea Logistics Center Detachment Portsmouth to address the FAR requirement to utilize PPI in source selections. OMB memo to all federal agencies encourages the use of PPIRS as the central governmentwide past performance retrieval database.	Established enduring system for accessing PPI. PPIRS was developed to give source selection officials a "one-stop shop" for retrieving potential suppliers' past performance history.
2004	DoD AT&L memo of December 17, 2007	DoD designates CPARS as its system of record for PP.	CPARS gained momentum toward widespread acceptance.
2005	D-2006-028 DoD Reporting System for the Competitive Sourcing Program. http://www.dodig.mil/audit/reports/FY06/06-028.txt	DoD Inspector General reports on the DoD Reporting System for the Competitive Sourcing Program.	Detailed limitations on PPI collection and use to monitor the cost of performance.

Year	Source/Report No.	Item	Impact
2007	Department of Defense Office of Inspector General, "Contractor Past Performance Information." Report No. D-2008-057, February 29, 2008. http://www.dodig.mil/Audit/reports/fy08/08-057.pdf	DoD CPARS system upgraded to allow automatic registration in CPARS from Federal Procurement Data System–Next Generation	Streamlined collection of PPI.
2007	GAO-07-1111T	*Federal Contracting: Use of Contractor Performance Information*	GAO described use of past performance as source selection factor and in monitoring contractor performance.
2008	Department of Defense Office of Inspector General. "Contractor Past Performance Information. "Report No. D-2008-057, February 29, 2008. http://www.dodig.mil/Audit/reports/fy08/08-057.pdf	U.S. Army transitions from Past Performance Information Management System (PPIMS) to CPARS	Movement toward CPARS as single collecton system for all agencies.
2008	D-2008-057	*Contractor Past Performance Information*	DoD Inspecter General conducted comprehensive review of past performance information.
2008	Duncan Hunter National Defense Authorization Act (P.L. 110-417), Sections 867 and 872	"Clean Contracting Act" mandates items to link performance with incentives and increase transparency of contractors' performance records	Required award fees to be paid only when a contractor has at least a satisfactory level of performance. Created a database for companies that have been suspended or disbarred (FAPIIS).
2009	GAO-09-374	*Better Performance Information Needed to Support Agency Contract Award Decisions*	GAO documented a comprehensive review of 62 solicitations and use of PPI.

Year	Source/Report No.	Item	Impact
2010	Supplemental Appropriations Act for Fiscal Year 2010 (P.L. 111-212), Section 3010. http://www.gpo.gov/fdsys/pkg/PLAW-111publ212/pdf/PLAW-111publ212.pdf	Amends 2008 Clean Contracting Act to require posting past performance information other than reviews on a publicly available Internet website	Mandated that FAPIIS information, except past performance reviews, submitted on or after April 15, 2011, be made publicly available.
2009	http://www.whitehouse.gov/sites/default/files/omb/assets/procurement/improving_use_of_contractor_perf_info.pdf	OFPP memorandum *Improving the Use of Contractor Performance Information*	OFPP required all agencies to make all contractor performance evaluations accessible in PPIRS.
2010	The Duncan Hunter National Defense Authorization Act of 2009 (Public Law 110-417)	Implementation of Federal Awardee Performance and Integrity Information System (FAPIIS)	System established that displays information regarding the integrity and performance of awardees of federal agency contracts and grants.
2010	Office of Federal Procurement Policy (OFPP) policy effective October 1, 2010	Designation of CPARS as governmentwide PPI entry point	CPARS became the governmentwide system for entering contractor past performance information into PPIRS.
2013	Section 806 of the 2012 National Defense Authorization Act, Section 853 of the 2013 National Defense Authorization Act implemented in FAR 42.1503	Shortened contractor response times to CPARS reports	Revised contractor response time to comment on CPARS from 30 to 14 days before CPARs report is uploaded into PPIRS.
2013	*Federal Register*, Vol. 78, No. 152. http://www.gpo.gov/fdsys/pkg/FR-2013-08-07/pdf/2013-18955.pdf	FAR Case 2012-028 as implemented in FAR 42.15, "Contractor Performance Information"	Standardized evaluation factors for past performance and adjectival rating scheme, as well as providing additional details on past performance evaluation and use of PPI.

Year	Source/Report No.	Item	Impact
2011-2013	See CPARS release history. https://www.cpars.gov/main/cparsrel.htm	Multiple revisions/updates to CPARS	CPARS made less "DoD-centric," user guides and system revised to reflect changes to FAR.
2014	*Federal Register*, Vol. 78, No. 68. http://www.gpo.gov/fdsys/pkg/FR-2013-04-09/pdf/2013-08190.pdf	Navy establishes Superior Supplier Incentive Program	Codified a supplier recognition program that draws from information in CPARS.

Chapter 2

THE PAST PERFORMANCE CYCLE

- →

Envisioning past performance as a cycle of activities helps to illustrate its potential power as a self-reinforcing process. By generating feedback that can be used to improve performance, these activities can improve contract outcomes and increase chances of business growth. As used by both buyer and seller, the past performance cycle includes some form of information collection, analogous processes of interpretation or evaluation, and a point or phase in the cycle we will call "use." These cycles operate continuously and incorporate many levels of activity, including purchases, projects, project phases, and incentives.

The past performance activities of buyers and sellers follow different cycles. As depicted here, the seller past performance cycle is more of a closed loop than the buyer past performance cycle, primarily because contract performance was taken out of the buyer cycle but left in the seller cycle. This was done to emphasize the primary role of the seller in contract performance. It is, admittedly, somewhat simplistic, in that the buyer can and does play an important role in contract performance—for example, by providing access to resources critical to contract performance. In truth, this is a shared responsibility; nonetheless, the emphasis is on the seller for performance.

The two cycles also overlap in several ways. External inputs and activities that take place outside the cycles impact each cycle, and both buyer and seller collect from the same sources and inputs, such as a person completing a past performance questionnaire or CPARS report. Additionally, the cycles overlap in the sense that ideally, both buyer and seller are interested in improving performance. Finally, both cycles feed back into themselves.

BUYER PAST PERFORMANCE CYCLE

At a high level, the buyer uses past performance information to assess performance: How has this party performed in the past? These assessments are most commonly part of source selection during a competitive procurement. A clear understanding of the buyer's process for obtaining, evaluating, and using past performance information is essential to sellers as they develop responses to solicitations, because they seek to showcase their past performance in all potential sources the buyer might turn to for information about their past performance. Buyers also should, naturally, be aware of their own agency's processes. The buyer past performance cycle is shown in Figure 2-1. (Not shown directly is the storage or retention of past performance information.)

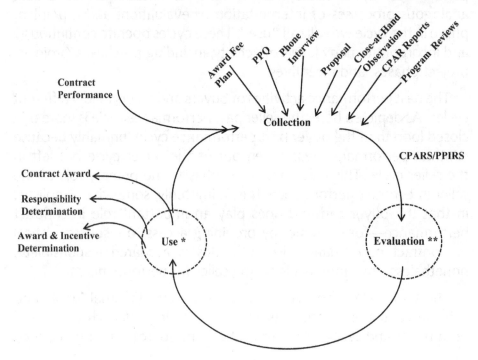

Figure 2-1: Buyer Past Performance Cycle

Contract award and *contract performance* are shown as output of and input to, respectively, the buyer past performance cycle. The term *contract award* means that the government has given notification that it is entering a contract with a private party. This may have been an award decision where one or more bidders learned they did not receive contract awards, or it may have been an award decision where there was only one bidder. For sellers, a contract award is the desired outcome from the buyer's use of past performance information in source selection (the process of determining which offeror to choose to make a contract award to among a group of offerors or other alternatives).

Bidding on and subsequently being awarded a contract means that contract performance information now starts accumulating experience that can be converted to past performance information. Thus begins the cycle: collection, evaluation, and use. Bidding on and subsequently *not* being awarded a contract means that *no* contract performance experience that can be used in the future as past performance information will be accumulated.

Collection

Sellers that do business with the federal government are usually familiar with its three main collection methods: past performance write-ups submitted as part of proposals, past performance questionnaires (PPQs) collected as part of a solicitation response, and contractor performance assessment reports (CPARs) collected during and after contract performance. Past performance information is not solely provided by the bidder and may come from multiple sources.

These sources can have a large impact on an evaluation outcome. Government agencies that frequently buy commercial items and place a significant number of orders under Federal Supply Schedules, governmentwide acquisition contracts, or other task order contracts may conclude that their quest to award contracts to good performers over good proposal writers is better served by evaluations that rely only on past performance and price, and not on extensive technical or management proposals. For a firm competing for work under this scenario, any individual source of past performance information can rise to a critical level when the buyer is deliberating on which firm will receive a contract. Table 2-1 summarizes all the collection methods used by government agencies and when/how past performance data are commonly recorded, used, and retained for later use.

Persistent problems regarding past performance can be categorized as stemming primarily from inputs and from organization. Persistent input problems arise from agencies not completing past performance reports, evaluators avoiding writing narratives, evaluators giving high scores rather than using evaluations to provide meaningful feedback, and written narratives that don't match or support assigned grades. Additional input problems come from the continued and pervasive use of burdensome collection methods, namely ad hoc, short-fused, and unpredictable (to the party completing them) paper-based past performance questionnaires.

Persistent organization problems regarding past performance come from continued use of a burdensome and disjointed collection, retention, and retrieval system for past performance information. Information is difficult to access, access is limited to a small population of users out of a potentially broader user base, and access is parsed and stovepiped so that the user experience is poor and utility derived from the system is low.

How Collected	How Recorded	When Used	How Used	Where Stored After Use
Proposal	As part of proposal	When bidders propose to perform work	Used to evaluate proposals.	In preaward contract file
Questionnaire	On past performance questionnaire (PPQ) form	As part of proposal response in some cases	Used to evaluate proposals.	In preaward contract file
Dun & Bradstreet Open Ratings	In Open Ratings evaluation summary report	As part of proposal response in some cases	Used to evaluate proposals.	In preaward contract file and available for one year from Dun & Bradstreet Open Ratings

How Collected	How Recorded	When Used	How Used	Where Stored After Use
Phone interview	Varied: notes of call or on PPQ or similar form	As part of proposal evaluation in some cases	Used to evaluate proposals.	In preaward contract file if documented and retained
Email response	In email body	As part of proposal evaluation in some cases	Used to evaluate proposals.	In preaward contract file if retained
Award fee plan report	Varied: per Award Fee Plan guidance for specific contract.	As required by Award Fee Plan in award fee contracts	Used to document performance during a specific contract period and form the basis for an award fee amount paid to contractor.	In contract file
Close-at-hand observation	Not generally recorded	As part of proposal evaluation in some cases	Used to evaluate proposals.	In preaward contract file if documented
Contractor performance assessment report (CPAR)	On CPAR form	As part of proposal or performance evaluation in some cases	Used to document performance during specific contract period. Can be used during proposal evaluations.	Uploaded into CPARS, fed into Past Performance Information Retrieval System (in future to be fed into System for Award Management)
Program review	Varied: may not be recorded	During contract performance	Program review may generate information regarding contractor performance during a contract period or periods.	Might not be recorded or retained

Table 2-1: Buyer Past Performance Information Collection Methods

These persistent issues contribute to a longstanding critique that the past performance information collected by an agency or activity is not made available to others (either within the agency or outside it) and therefore is not used by other agencies or activities in making procurement decisions. This criticism holds true across collection methods despite many years of attempts to address this fundamental problem. In 2006, the General Services Administration observed the following concerning past performance and its nuances:

> It has long been a vulnerability that Government agencies would award to a vendor who owes another part of the Government money or services, or is in the process of being debarred. This was due to the fact that information about performance was maintained at the local contracting office level. (GSA, 2006)

A brief discussion of each method and its impact on data usage and retention/retrieval follows.

Proposal

Bidders submit past performance information in proposals, typically in a separate section or volume from the proposal itself, and otherwise as directed in the solicitation. The information collected is used for proposal evaluation. A proposal consists of an offer or promise of work, price or cost information, and information about the bidder (Figure 2-2). Past performance information is part of the information about the bidder *(proposer capability information)*. This information can be provided (as directed in the solicitation) in a variety of formats, most commonly written information and oral presentations.

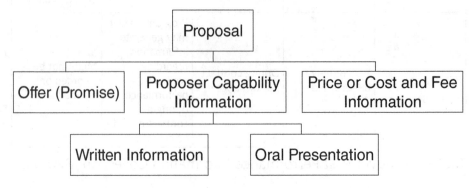

Figure 2-2: Components of a Proposal

Past performance information collected in proposals typically goes no further than the preaward contract file, whether paper or electronic. These files generally are not searchable or electronically archived in any manner conducive to access or use for any other purpose.

Past Performance Questionnaire

PPQs are typically collected as part of a proposal response and used during proposal evaluation. Solicitations provide guidance on how they are to be completed and returned to the contracting officer or other government official. The norm is to include a specific PPQ form in the solicitation. This form is not filled out by the bidder but sent by the bidder to several client references of their choice, who are asked to return the completed form directly to the contracting officer or designee. PPQs collected during preaward typically go no further than preaward contract files, which generally are not searchable or electronically archived in any manner conducive to access or use for any other purpose.

Dun & Bradstreet Open Ratings Report

For a fee, Open Ratings, Inc. (a Dun & Bradstreet company), conducts an independent audit of customer references and calculates a rating based on statistical analysis of various performance data and survey responses. Some agencies, notably the General Services Administration (GSA) for Federal Supply Schedule proposals, use Open Ratings for collecting past performance information in proposals and for evaluating past performance during proposal evaluation.

The performance data collected in the Open Ratings survey is provided in an Open Ratings evaluation report and includes customer ratings on a contractor's overall performance, reliability, cost, order accuracy, delivery/timeliness, quality, business relations, personnel, customer support, and responsiveness. The solicitation directs sellers to file with Open Ratings and show evidence of this filing (to include, in some cases, a copy of the evaluation report).

Aside from firm identification data, the primary information supplied to Open Ratings by a seller is contact information for 20 client references. Open Ratings considers four responses from these references to be the minimum needed to complete a rating and declares its past performance evaluation reports to be valid for one year. The soliciting agency will most likely retain Open Ratings reports along with proposals in the preaward contract file. They are also kept on file and are accessible (for a fee) directly from Open Ratings during the one-year validity period.

Phone Interview

Phone interviews are occasionally conducted by contracting officers and designees as a part of past performance evaluation during a proposal evaluation for source selection purposes. Phone interviews may be conducted using a standard set of questions—in essence, a PPQ form.

In an evaluation of past performance, there is no legal requirement that a government agency must contact all the references submitted by a particular bidder. But the agency must act reasonably when it decides which references to contact or not contact: Government agencies must make a reasonable effort to make contact, and if that reasonable effort does not result in contact with the reference, the agency can complete its evaluation without the reference.

When instructed to provide contact information for its past performance references in a proposal, a prudent bidder will include references familiar with it that will respond to queries in a timely fashion and provide a good reference. Many agencies ask for both a technical and a contracts reference for each cited past contract performance. In some cases, *only* contact information is requested (i.e., no past performance write-up).

Phone interviews may be recorded as call notes or on a PPQ (or similar) form. The notes are most likely to be retained in the preaward contract file, with the same level of access as for PPQ questionnaires.

Email Response

Similar to phone interviews, email responses may be used as part of proposal evaluation and may be solicited directly from the past performance references provided by bidders using a set of questions or a PPQ template. Email responses are recorded in the email body or as an attachment and may be retained in preaward contract files.

Award or Incentive Plan Report

Award fee plans (used in award fee contracts) provide guidance on the collection of performance information for specified contract periods. This past performance information is typically collected in a standard response format (as specified by each plan) that, ideally, contains elements tying important contract objectives to the incentives or awards in the contract. This information is used to determine award fee amounts during and following contract performance; it is kept in the contract files, which are not typically archived or stored electronically in a manner conducive to later retrieval.

FAR 42.1503 was revised in September 2013 to specifically state that incentive and award fee performance information is to be included in past performance ratings and evaluations entered into CPARS. This FAR language does not state that CPARS evaluation reports are to be produced coincident with award and incentive fee plan evaluations of contractor performance and does not apply to procedures used by agencies in determining fees under award or incentive fee contracts. When past performance of an award or incentive fee contract is evaluated, this element of contract performance is to be rated as part of any CPARs covering the same period, using the adjectival rating scale provided by the same FAR section (see "Evaluation"). It also sets the expectation that the fee amount paid to contractors under award or incentive fee arrangements should reflect the contractor's performance and the past performance evaluation should closely parallel and be consistent with the fee determinations.

Close-at-Hand Observation

When agency or government staff directly observe contractor performance, this is referred to as *close-at-hand observation*. Although this type of past performance information is not generally captured or recorded, it is an established precedent in case law that close-at-hand observation of contractor performance cannot be ignored during source selection evaluations (see for example GAO B-280511.2, GTS Duratek, Inc., 1998,[7] and GAO B-401679.4 et al., Shaw-Parsons Infrastructure Recovery Consultants, LLC and Vanguard Recovery Assistance, Joint Venture, 2010[8]) and, if it exists, must be used during proposal evaluations. GAO review precedent is that this information should be considered the same as any other past performance information presented by the seller or found by the buyer.

Some agencies and activities purposefully and systematically collect close-at-hand contract performance information, but the majority do not. The likely means of collection and retention of this type of past performance information, if it is documented, is in any evaluation working papers or decision documents retained in the preaward contract files.

CPARS Reports

CPARS reports are collected periodically as described in Chapter 4. CPARS forms are sometimes reviewed during proposal evaluation or as a reference when completing performance evaluations during contract performance.

The standardization, retention, and retrieval provided by CPARS is intended to make records of past performance information accessible across agencies for the purpose of evaluating contractor past performance. Currently, these records are accessible via CPARS and the Past Performance Information Retrieval System (PPIRS). A planned update to the System for Award Management (SAM) will include the information in PPIRS in SAM. Past performance information in CPARS reports is retained for three years.

Program Review

It is a best practice for government programs to periodically conduct some form of a program review. There is no specified form or format for such review that is universally applicable, and this type of past

---

[7] www.gao.gov/products/402719#mt=e-report.

[8] www.gao.gov/assets/390/388459.pdf.

performance information is not likely to be recorded or retained. These reviews may generate past performance information regarding contractor performance during a contract period or periods.

Use of this information is similar to that described for close-at-hand observation. It is unlikely that this information would be retained in any way that is searchable or accessible outside the office that generated the review.

Evaluation

Evaluation refers to a buyer's evaluation of a bidder's past performance against stated evaluation criteria.

In the solicitation, the agency is required to describe the evaluation approach it will follow and provide an opportunity for bidders to identify past or current contracts that they performed on and to detail any problems encountered and corrective actions taken. The evaluation of past performance must consider the currency and relevance of the information, the source and context of the information, and general trends in contractor performance. The government *must* consider information from the offeror and other sources and *should* consider information about predecessor companies, key personnel, and subcontractors.

As described in Chapter 1, three standard rules in the government's evaluation of past performance are that (1) If no record of *relevant* past performance exists, the offeror may not be evaluated either favorably or unfavorably on past performance; (2) the offeror must be provided the opportunity to address adverse past performance information that it has not previously had an opportunity to comment on; and (3) the government cannot reveal the names of *individuals* providing reference information about an offeror's past performance.

In addition to these three standards, what is to be evaluated and how it is to be evaluated must be stated in the solicitation, and when conducting the evaluation this "what and how" must be followed. (This information is in Section M of the solicitation.) Typically, the stated evaluation scheme will specify the evaluation criteria for the past performance itself, along with how the relevance of the past performance will be evaluated. Evaluation criteria for past performance may include things such as the management performance of the specified relevant past performance, the quality of the products or services delivered, how well schedule requirements were adhered to, and the cost control performance of the specified relevant contracts cited as past performance. Relevance of past performance information can take into consideration such things as the nature of the business areas involved, the required levels of technology, contract types, similarity of materials and products, location of work to be performed, and similarity in size, scope, and complexity.

The government's basic objective regarding past performance evaluation is to measure the level of confidence in an offeror's ability to successfully perform based on previous and current contract performance data. This level of confidence is expressed in a performance risk assessment, in which evaluators assign an adjectival rating based on their evaluation of the offeror's past performance. A typical adjectival rating scheme for assessing performance risk based on past performance is shown in Table 2-2. A thorough past performance evaluation, by including reviewing information from sources in addition to those submitted in a proposal, ensures that awards are made to good performers over good proposal writers.

Adjective	Description
Low Risk	Based on offeror's past performance record, essentially no doubt exists that the offeror will successfully perform the required effort.
Moderate Risk	Based on offeror's past performance record, some doubt exists that the offeror will successfully perform the required effort.
High Risk	Based on offeror's past performance record, extreme doubt exists that the offeror will successfully perform the required effort.
Unknown Risk	No relevant performance record upon which to base a meaningful performance risk prediction is identifiable.

Table 2-2: Adjectival Rating Scheme for Assessing Performance Risk Based on Past Performance

An important and often misunderstood differentiation between past performance and experience can come into play during evaluation. As stated above, government agencies are not allowed to unfavorably evaluate bidders with no past performance. This is sometimes referred to as the *neutral rule*, because a bidder with no past performance is to be evaluated neutrally (not negatively) on past performance. However, agencies *can* negatively evaluate a bidder's *experience* if it has no past performance, if the solicitation makes this distinction.

GAO protest decisions are based in part on how the solicitation is written. If no distinction is made between experience and past performance in the solicitation, the decision normally is that the two elements cannot be evaluated separately. If a clear distinction is made in the solicitation between past performance and experience, then a bidder can be evaluated separately on these two elements, and a bidder with no past performance and no relevant experience could be evaluated neutrally on past performance and negatively on experience. The majority of solicitations and evaluation schemes are not this clear, however, and the terms *past performance* and *experience* are often conflated or used interchangeably in solicitations.

Past performance evaluation as a part of source selection for award of a contract can take place as a prequalification, as in a two-step or other phased source selection process. For example, a first round of past performance and capability information submission could result in a down-select decision by the buying agency that limits the final or subsequent participation in this acquisition to a subset of the interested respondents.

Evaluation of a company's past performance also takes place outside source selection evaluations: during program reviews, during the completion of CPARS reports, during award or incentive fee determinations, and at other less formal times during or after contract performance. These are shown in the expansion of the "evaluation" area of the buyer past performance cycle shown in Figure 2-3.

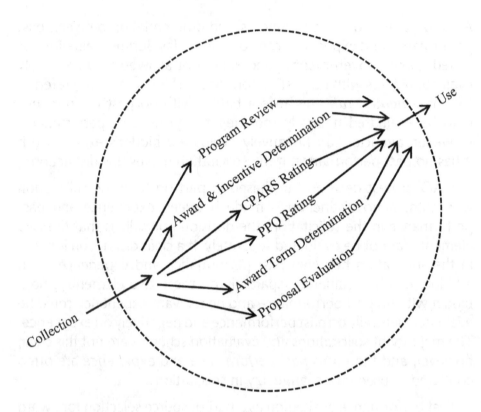

Figure 2-3: Evaluation, Buyer Past Performance Cycle

Historically, a higher level of scrutiny is applied to—and a higher degree of compliance is achieved in—the form, format, and procedures that are used during source selections, when an agency determines to which offeror among a group of offerors it will award a contract. At other times, however, such as evaluating contractor performance during contract performance or assessing bidder past performance in a responsibility determinations, less oversight and attention has been paid. It is in part because of this that several issues with past performance evaluation persist across government agencies (GAO, 2009). First, past performance evaluations (or contractor evaluations during contract performance) are not always completed. Second, even when completed, evaluations either are cursory or fail to provide direct, actionable, or constructive critiques on performance. Third, opportunities to collect and retain past performance information and information on contractor performance are missed, and past performance information repositories are thus rendered ineffective at best. Weaknesses in the collection, retention, and use of past performance information have been repeatedly decried by oversight and other organizations such as GAO, inspectors general, and industry groups. Some government agencies have dramatically improved their past performance information collection efforts, particularly via CPARS. (It is worth noting that CPARS is for unclassified information only, and intelligence community agencies largely do not use CPARS.)

Additionally, FAR 42.15 on contractor performance information was revised in September 2013 to detail when, where, what, how, and by whom contractor performance is to be evaluated. The *when* is annually and when contract performance is completed. The *where* is electronically in CPARS, from which data are automatically migrated to PPIRS after 14 days. The *who* includes the technical office, contracting office, program management office, and, where appropriate, quality assurance and end users of the product or service who provide inputs to evaluations. If a specific person is not designated as being responsible for completing the evaluation (e.g., contracting officer, contracting officer's representative, project manager, program manager) the contracting officer is the party responsible for the evaluation.

The *what* is first established in FAR 42.15 by defining *past performance information* as relevant information, for future source selection purposes, regarding a contractor's actions under previously awarded contracts or orders and includes the contractor's record of

1. Conforming to requirements and standards of good workmanship
2. Forecasting and controlling costs
3. Adherence to schedules, including the administrative aspects of performance
4. Reasonable and cooperative behavior and commitment to customer satisfaction
5. Reporting into databases
6. Integrity and business ethics
7. Businesslike concern for the interest of the customer.

The *how* is by using standardized adjectival rating schemes and specified elements of past performance information to be reviewed and evaluated. Required evaluation factors include (at a minimum):

1. Technical quality of product or service

2. Cost control (not applicable for firm fixed-price or fixed-price with economic price adjustment arrangements)

3. Schedule/timeliness

4. Management or business relations

5. Small business subcontracting (as applicable)

6. Other (as applicable—e.g., late or nonpayment to subcontractors, trafficking violations, tax delinquency, failure to report in accordance with contract terms and conditions, defective cost or pricing data, terminations, suspensions, debarments).

These factors can include subfactors, and each factor and subfactor is required to both be evaluated and have a supporting narrative. The evaluation rating scale and definitions are shown in Figures 2-4 and 2-5, reproduced directly from FAR Tables 42-1 (for prime contractor performance) and 42-2 (for small business and subcontracting performance).

Rating	Definition	Note
Exceptional	Performance meets contractual requirements and exceeds many to the Government's benefit. The contractual performance of the element or sub-element being evaluated was accomplished with few minor problems for which corrective actions taken by the contractor were highly effective.	To justify an Exceptional rating, identify multiple significant events and state how they were of benefit to the Government. A singular benefit, however, could be of such magnitude that it alone constitutes an Exceptional rating. Also, there should have been NO significant weaknesses identified.
Very Good	Performance meets contractual requirements and exceeds some to the Government's benefit. The contractual performance of the element or sub-element being evaluated was accomplished with some minor problems for which corrective actions taken by the contractor were effective	To justify a Very Good rating, identify a significant event and state how it was a benefit to the Government. There should have been no significant weaknesses identified.

Rating	Definition	Note
Satisfactory	Performance meets contractual requirements. The contractual performance of the element or sub-element contains some minor problems for which corrective actions taken by the contractor appear or were satisfactory.	To justify a Satisfactory rating, there should have been only minor problems, or major problems the contractor recovered from without impact to the contract/order. There should have been NO significant weaknesses identified. A fundamental principle of assigning ratings is that contractors will not be evaluated with a rating lower than Satisfactory solely for not performing beyond the requirements of the contract/order.
Marginal	Performance does not meet some contractual requirements. The contractual performance of the element or sub-element being evaluated reflects a serious problem for which the contractor has not yet identified corrective actions. The contractor's proposed actions appear only marginally effective or were not fully implemented.	To justify Marginal performance, identify a significant event in each category that the contractor had trouble overcoming and state how it impacted the Government. A Marginal rating should be supported by referencing the management tool that notified the contractor of the contractual deficiency (e.g., management, quality, safety, or environmental deficiency report or letter).
Unsatisfactory	Performance does not meet most contractual requirements and recovery in a timely manner is not likely. The contractual performance of the element or sub-element contains a serious problem(s) for which the contractor's corrective actions appear or were ineffective.	To justify an Unsatisfactory rating, identify multiple significant events in each category that the contractor had trouble overcoming and state how it impacted the Government. A singular problem, however, could be of such serious magnitude that it alone constitutes an unsatisfactory rating. An Unsatisfactory rating should be supported by referencing the management tools used to notify the contractor of the contractual deficiencies (e.g., management, quality, safety, or environmental deficiency reports, or letters).

Figure 2-4: Past Performance Evaluation Rating and Definitions from FAR Table 42-1

NOTE 1: Plus or minus signs may be used to indicate an improving (+) or worsening (-) trend insufficient to change the evaluation status.

NOTE 2: N/A (not applicable) should be used if the ratings are not going to be applied to a particular area for evaluation.

Rating	Definition	Note
Exceptional	Exceeded all statutory goals or goals as negotiated. Had exceptional success with initiatives to assist, promote, and utilize small business (SB), small disadvantaged business (SDB), women-owned small business (WOSB), HUBZone small business, veteran-owned small business (VOSB) and service disabled veteran owned small business (SDVOSB). Complied with FAR 52.219-8, Utilization of Small Business Concerns. Exceeded any other small business participation requirements incorporated in the contract/order, including the use of small businesses in mission critical aspects of the program. Went above and beyond the required elements of the subcontracting plan and other small business requirements of the contract/order. Completed and submitted Individual Subcontract Reports and/or Summary Subcontract Reports in an accurate and timely manner.	To justify an Exceptional rating, identify multiple significant events and state how they were a benefit to small business utilization. A singular benefit, however, could be of such magnitude that it constitutes an Exceptional rating. Small businesses should be given meaningful and innovative work directly related to the contract, and opportunities should not be limited to indirect work such as cleaning offices, supplies, landscaping, etc. Also, there should have been no significant weaknesses identified.
Very Good	Met all of the statutory goals or goals as negotiated. Had significant success with initiatives to assist, promote and utilize SB, SDB, WOSB, HUBZone, VOSB, and SDVOSB. Complied with FAR 52.219-8, Utilization of Small Business Concerns. Met or exceeded any other small business participation requirements incorporated in the contract/order, including the use of small businesses in mission critical aspects of the program. Endeavored to go above and beyond the required elements of the subcontracting plan. Completed and submitted Individual Subcontract Reports and/or Summary Subcontract Reports in an accurate and timely manner.	To justify a Very Good rating, identify a significant event and state how it was a benefit to small business utilization. Small businesses should be given meaningful and innovative opportunities to participate as subcontractors for work directly related to the contract, and opportunities should not be limited to indirect work such as cleaning offices, supplies, landscaping, etc. There should be no significant weaknesses identified.

Rating	Definition	Note
Satisfactory	Demonstrated a good faith effort to meet all of the negotiated subcontracting goals in the various socio-economic categories for the current period. Complied with FAR 52.219-8, Utilization of Small Business Concerns. Met any other small business participation requirements included in the contract/order. Fulfilled the requirements of the subcontracting plan included in the contract/order. Completed and submitted Individual Subcontract Reports and/or Summary Subcontract Reports in an accurate and timely manner.	To justify a Satisfactory rating, there should have been only minor problems, or major problems the contractor has addressed or taken corrective action. There should have been no significant weaknesses identified. A fundamental principle of assigning ratings is that contractors will not be assessed a rating lower than Satisfactory solely for not performing beyond the requirements of the contract/order.
Marginal	Deficient in meeting key subcontracting plan elements. Deficient in complying with FAR 52.219-8, Utilization of Small Business Concerns, and any other small business participation requirements in the contract/order. Did not submit Individual Subcontract Reports and/or	To justify Marginal performance, identify a significant event that the contractor had trouble overcoming and how it impacted small business utilization. A Marginal rating should be supported by referencing the actions taken by the government that notified the contractor of the contractual deficiency.
	Summary Subcontract Reports in an accurate or timely manner. Failed to satisfy one or more requirements of a corrective action plan currently in place; however, does show an interest in bringing performance to a satisfactory level and has demonstrated a commitment to apply the necessary resources to do so. Required a corrective action plan.	

Rating	Definition	Note
Unsatisfactory	Noncompliant with FAR 52.219-8 and 52.219-9, and any other small business participation requirements in the contract/order. Did not submit Individual Subcontract Reports and/or Summary Subcontract Reports in an accurate or timely manner. Showed little interest in bringing performance to a satisfactory level or is generally uncooperative. Required a corrective action plan.	To justify an Unsatisfactory rating, identify multiple significant events that the contractor had trouble overcoming and state how it impacted small business utilization. A singular problem, however, could be of such serious magnitude that it alone constitutes an Unsatisfactory rating. An Unsatisfactory rating should be supported by referencing the actions taken by the government to notify the contractor of the deficiencies. When an Unsatisfactory rating is justified, the contracting officer must consider whether the contractor made a good faith effort to comply with the requirements of the subcontracting plan required by FAR 52.219-9 and follow the procedures outlined in FAR 52.219-16, Liquidated Damages-Subcontracting Plan.

Figure 2-5: Small Business Subcontracting Past Performance Evaluation Rating and Definitions from FAR Table 42-2

NOTE 1: Plus or minus signs may be used to indicate an improving (+) or worsening (-) trend insufficient to change evaluation status.

NOTE 2: Generally, zero percent is not a goal unless the contracting officer determined when negotiating the subcontracting plan that no subcontracting opportunities exist in a particular socio-economic category. In such cases, the contractor shall be considered to have met the goal for any socioeconomic category where the goal negotiated in the plan was zero.

Evaluation of past performance information typically precedes its storage and retention—that is, it is not stored or retained unless it has been evaluated. The implication of this statement is that past performance information exists in two forms: information that *has* been evaluated and information that *has not* been evaluated. An example of the former is the formal documentation (including the evaluation) of a contractor's performance in a CPARS report. This evaluated past performance information has a high likelihood of being captured and retained in a past performance repository.

An example of the latter is information generated during a program review conducted in an agency. This illustrative program review likely was conducted using a locally devised framework and may or may not include judgmental evaluations of contractor performance. Therefore, it could include past performance information that has not been evaluated. The likelihood of this unevaluated past performance information being captured and retained in a past performance information repository of any sort is extremely low. Contractors should be aware of this occurrence and apply the same management principles recommended for evaluated past performance information. Government agencies should likewise take advantage of this past performance information.

One could argue that unevaluated past performance information regarding contract awards, dollar amounts, and so on, such as can be found in sites or systems like the Federal Funding Accountability and Transparency Act site, on the USAspending.gov site, in the System for Award Management (SAM), or in the Federal Procurement Data System, are past performance information repositories. While this is a true statement, the extremely abbreviated and encoded nature of these repositories makes them unsuitable for past performance evaluations.

Storage and Retention

The primary repository of past performance information used by the government is CPARS. All data in CPARS are to be accessible (per FAR Part 42) in PPIRS to agencies.

Government agencies are required by regulation to document contractor performance. A more recent addition to the requirements to store and retain past performance information is the requirement to document terminations for cause or default, determination of contractor fault by DoD, determinations of non-responsibility, and defective cost or pricing data in the Federal Awardee Performance and Integrity Information System (FAPIIS). Grant issuers and administrators are also charged with documenting "recipient not qualified" determinations and terminations for material failure to comply in FAPIIS. Storage of past performance information is covered in more detail in Chapter 4.

Use

At a high level, the buyer uses past performance information to assess performance: How has this firm performed in the past? These assessments are most frequently used and thought of as part of source selection during a competitive procurement (as described in Evaluation).

The purpose of using past performance information, from the buyer's perspective, is twofold: First, to make sound business decisions during contractor selection and during contract performance. Second, to provide feedback to contractors to improve overall contract performance. These purposes are fulfilled during the "use" section of the buyer's past performance cycle (Figure 2-6). A discussion of the three uses—responsibility determination, source selection, and award or incentive determination—follows.

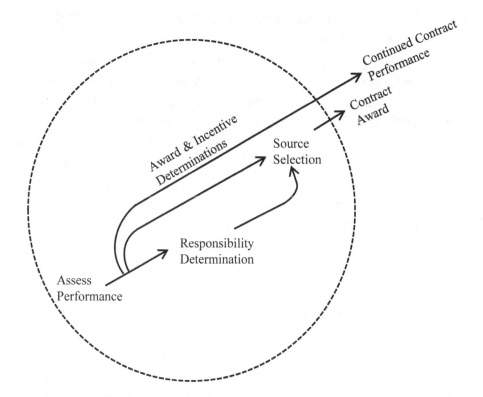

Figure 2-6: Use, Buyer Past Performance Cycle

Responsibility Determination

The FAR uses the term *responsible* to describe an offeror that has the capability, tenacity, and perseverance to perform a particular contract. Every contract award must have a determination of responsibility. A contracting officer signing an awarded contract signifies the affirmative determination that the contractor is responsible.

Before awarding a contract, a contracting officer conducts a responsibility determination. An affirmative *responsibility determination* is when a government agency (i.e., a contracting officer) concludes that an offeror is in fact an *acceptable* contract awardee. At this point, multiple offerors may be responsible.

A responsibility determination is different from a source selection evaluation, which is the process of determining *which* offeror to choose to make a contract award to among a group of offerors or other alternatives. Award of any contract, often done without a formal source selection process (e.g., a sole source contract award or a small purchase), always requires a positive responsibility determination.

The Small Business Administration may get involved (likely at the request of a small business offeror that was determined to be non-responsible by a contracting officer) and may issue a certificate of responsibility called a *certificate of competency*. In fact, this certificate can override a non-responsibility finding by the awarding agency.

The past performance of a prospective contractor is one element considered during this process. A responsibility determination is a subjective determination made based on seven factors:

1. Have or can get adequate financial resources to perform
2. Have or can get capacity to perform
3. Have a satisfactory performance record (i.e., past performance)
4. Have a satisfactory record of ethics and integrity (i.e., past performance)
5. Have or can get needed business and performance skills to perform
6. Have or can get needed facilities to perform
7. Be qualified and eligible under applicable laws and regulations.

The best evidence for satisfying that a business "has or can get" these elements is that it has successfully used them on other government contracts similar in size, scope, and complexity—in effect, that it has satisfactory past performance in all seven areas.

Source Selection

Source selection is the most recognizable use of past performance information by the government, being the use most often considered in discussing the use of past performance by government agencies. This use is covered in detail in Chapter 5 on past performance evaluations.

Award Fee, Award Term, and Incentive Determinations

Award and incentive fee arrangements used in award and incentive type contracts are intended to:

- Provide for assessments of contractor performance levels
- Focus the contractor on areas of greatest importance
- Communicate assessment procedures and thus government priorities
- Provide for effective, two-way communication between the contractor and evaluators
- Provide for an equitable and timely assessment process
- Establish an effective organizational structure to administer award fee provisions.

Retrospective performance (i.e., *recent* past performance or performance during the contract award or incentive period just completed) is the primary factor in an award or incentive determination. *Award fee, award term,* and *incentive* refer to the specific contract types requiring these determinations. The contract will specify (or should specify) the performance assessment criteria, the periodicity, and other aspects of the administration of the award or incentive. These matters are covered in an award or incentive fee determination plan included as an addendum to the contract.

Incentives and awards can be either subjective or objective. For objective plans, typically associated with incentive-fee arrangements, there is less likely to be an evaluation of past performance as part of the administration of the plan. In subjective plans, typically associated with an award fee or award term plan, there is a high likelihood that subjective measures will be defined in the contract and contractor performance will be assessed against these criteria to determine the amount of the award.

These contract types are less frequently used but do generate past performance information that must be documented and stored. As of the September 2013 rewrite of FAR 42.1500, these performance assessments are required to be captured in CPARS, will thus be retained in PPIRS, and will be available for either six years (for construction and architect-engineer contracts) or three years (for all other contracts) for agencies to review as part of past performance evaluations during source selection.

Award fee determinations are unilateral decisions by the government, even though a best practice in award fee determination plans is to have the contractor perform a self-assessment and provide input during the review cycle. Award fees are typically paid in three- to six-month increments, so an award or incentive fee contract can generate a number of award fee determinations as well as past performance evaluation content in CPARS over the life of the contract.

SELLER PAST PERFORMANCE CYCLE

The seller past performance cycle is shown in Figure 2-7. Sellers that desire to perform well collect and use past and current performance information to stay informed about their performance, monitor and take corrective action as needed to improve performance, measure progress against goals, and revise measures and goals as needed. They also collect and manage past performance information for more purposes than just using it in their next proposal, such as for employee feedback or as part of a performance improvement program. This focus on continually improving performance, combined with ensuring that performance records reflect positively on their past performance, meshes with the government goal of using past performance information to improve contractor performance.

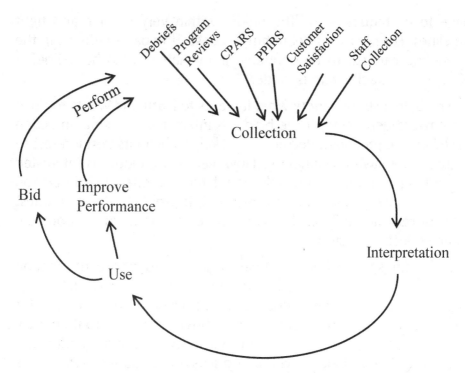

Figure 2-7: Seller Past Performance Cycle

Collection

Sellers collect past performance information from a variety of sources, including debriefings (both unsuccessful offers and awarded contract proposal debriefings), program reviews, CPARS reports, and customer satisfaction surveys and programs, as well as that information collected by staff performing or monitoring their own firm's performance.

Debriefings

Debriefings are feedback from a buyer to a seller when a contract decision is made. Typically this is a contract award decision, and the seller may or may not be the awardee; other decisions by the government also can provide the basis for a debriefing, such as exclusion from the competitive range or otherwise being excluded from competition before an award. A FAR precept is that debriefings have to be requested by the bidder within very specific and tight timelines. For preaward debriefing requests, the party requesting the debriefing can ask to be debriefed immediately or to be debriefed after the contract award is made.

The bidder should know what it wants to learn and wants to do in a preaward debriefing. If the bidder is interested in taking an action based on the preaward decision, it is likely to be in its best interest to request a preaward debriefing. However, if the bidder is interested in learning as much as possible about the eventual award decision but is unlikely to take immediate action, it probably should request a postaward debriefing. That way, more can be learned about the source selection decision.

Debriefings are an important part of past performance information collection. Sellers should take full advantage of every debriefing opportunity: They should request one at every opportunity, ask for and take advantage of in-person debriefings, and come to them fully prepared. Coming fully prepared means reviewing the solicitation and submitted proposal along with any discussion or clarification rounds that have occurred. Sellers should be aware of the varied viewpoints on the buyer side and seek direct participation and feedback from each viewpoint in the debriefing. These viewpoints include the contracting officer, the source selection authority, the technical evaluation team lead, or other evaluation teams (management, past performance, price, or other). Preparation includes coming to the conversation with a collection of questions and advance preparation by the direct participants (from the seller) in the debriefing. Feedback during a debriefing can and should include feedback on the competitive field, on the evaluation process, on the proposal, and on the rating of the proposal. Questions for consideration include:

- Was the successful offeror already performing work for the agency?
- What other firms are on the successful offeror's team?
- Who were the other offerors?
- What did the price and technical score distribution look like?

- Please describe the process by which evaluation scores were derived by the government evaluators.
- Please describe the makeup and composition of the evaluation team.
- Please provide a detailed breakdown of our technical score by proposal section, including detail on strengths and weaknesses.
- Please provide specific feedback on the subcontractor plan rating.
- Please describe the perceived strengths and weaknesses in our proposed incumbent personnel retention strategy.
- Please describe the perceived strengths and weaknesses in our proposed transition plan.
- What needed improvement in our proposal, or in the government assessment of the risk associated with an award to our firm; how could we have mitigated this perceived risk?
  - Company experience
  - Management approach
  - Facilities or geographic coverage
  - Key personnel
  - Proposed labor mix and utilization
  - Proposed technical solution
  - Qualifications of proposed personnel
  - Past performance.

As can be seen in this list of possible questions, a debriefing is an opportunity to obtain feedback on not only how the past performance was perceived and rated but also on other aspects of the firm's proposal that might affect how the firm is viewed.

Program Reviews

The term *program review* is used here to mean any review, formal or otherwise, conducted by an agency or client on the progress of a project or program. In projects and programs involving contracted support, it is normal for the review to include comments on contractor performance. These evaluations of performance are a potential collection point for a seller of how a particular buyer or agency views its performance.

These views of contractor performance are not likely to be stored in a searchable repository of past performance information, but they could form the basis for close-at-hand information about contractor performance or purposeful collection of past performance information at the activity or agency level on a specific project or program.

CPARS Reports

It is in a firm's best interest to proactively manage its CPARS reports. Firms are provided limited access to CPARS via individual, named account holders. A firm needs to assign an account access person who actively monitors postings and associated email notifications. Using an organizational mailbox with multiple recipients to ensure that email notifications are received and acted upon is useful if accountability for action is not lost in doing so. A firm should know which projects it has ongoing and when CPARS reports are or could be completed and should prompt its clients to complete the reports, to fully document the firm's performance, and to comment appropriately on the filed reports. It behooves a firm to collect and store its CPARS reports for its own use.

Customer Satisfaction Surveys

Customer satisfaction monitoring can be done in a variety of ways. Firms can and should collect customer satisfaction information on a regular, recurring basis. Conventional wisdom regarding this collection method is that the best results are achieved by using a neutral or objective third party to solicit and collect customer satisfaction data in a manner that makes it relatively easy for the customer to provide meaningful feedback. The methods to do this are varied and, compared to the highly scripted nature of CPARS, can be easily tailored to the type and depth of feedback sought, the disposition of the customer toward responding to queries, and the retention and dissemination of the information collected. Customer satisfaction and perceptions can be collected from existing, past, prospective, or representative customers.

Staff Collection

An often overlooked means of collecting past performance information and both client and self-perceptions of current performance is from a source that is perhaps closest to the client on a regular basis: the staff performing on current projects. Collection opportunities include normal daily interactions, the submission and review of recurring status reports, and program or project reviews. Firms that perform government work often default to or rely upon the government to specify the frequency and format of the program and project reviews where this type of information can arise and feedback collection can occur. Firms are well served by not missing these opportunities and by taking the initiative to schedule and conduct regular reviews, submit and follow up on performance feedback via recurring reports, and drive agendas during interactions with clients to obtain performance feedback with adequate specificity to inform service delivery and the management of client perceptions.

Interpretation

Unlike the government buyer, the seller is not guided by rule and regulation in the evaluation of its own past performance. Our choice of the term *interpretation* as opposed to *evaluation* reflects this distinction. (Evaluation of past performance information is covered in greater detail in Chapter 5.) The seller can choose to evaluate its own past performance against a grading scale or schema. For the purposes of proposals, it should evaluate its past performance information to select the past performance citations to use in a particular proposal, to choose whether to bid on a solicitation, and to determine how to best present its past performance information.

The seller needs to interpret the past performance information it receives, seeks out, collects, or otherwise encounters. This interpretation includes making sense of the information, both for itself and with the aim of predicting how others (e.g., buyers) will make sense of and evaluate the information—particularly for relevancy and scoring against proposal and CPARS evaluation criteria.

Of primary consideration in interpretation by a seller is the removal or overcoming of biases in its analysis. Collection sources and methods or channels each come with their own inherent lean toward a particular view or perspective. One bias that is pervasive and difficult to overcome is the strong emotional response of the party receiving feedback or past performance information when its own "blood, sweat, and tears" went into delivery of the goods or services. Additionally, the perceived value of the delivery team is highly likely to be graded, judged, compensated, or in some way affected by the nature of the past performance information it receives. Under these circumstances, it is human nature to selectively listen, to not be objective, to filter information, or to consider explaining or forming a retort instead of actively listening when confronted with feedback and information about past performance. This is particularly true when that feedback or information is critical or seemingly prepared and provided with little thought or effort.

Acknowledging, then, that it is difficult to predict how others will evaluate one's past performance, and also acknowledging persistent biases and filters between a performance and looking back at that performance through past performance information, how can the information be interpreted? One way is to submit it to a proxy for the eventual or actual evaluator(s), such as a person with similar attributes (e.g., used to work at the buyer agency, served in a role same as or similar to an expected evaluator, had similar experiences as an expected evaluator) to gain an understanding of the actual evaluator's potential disposition and considerations. Another method is to seek out direct feedback from prospective evaluators at times other than during a proposal evaluation. This feedback can be sought during formal and informal project and program performance reviews, during and following submission of status reports, in advance of a CPARS evaluation point, and during data collection as part of a customer satisfaction program.

Storage and Retention

Seller retention and storage of past performance information is not prescribed by any governing or regulatory guidance outside of the firm itself; therefore, there is a range of ways this is accomplished, from doing nothing in particular to store or manage past performance information to tightly controlling the storage and retention of past performance information using all manner of archiving and retrieval systems and topologies. This topic is covered in greater detail in Chapter 4.

Use

One way to think about how a firm manages its past performance is through the lens of an equation or model. Heskett, Sasser, and Schlesinger provide an equation for customer value (1997):

$$\text{Value} = \frac{\text{Results Produced for the Customer} + \text{Process Quality}}{\text{Price to the Customer} + \text{Costs of Acquiring the Service}}$$

They use this equation to illustrate that value to the customer is a function of both results achieved and quality of service offset against the price and other costs associated with acquiring the service. In this model, managing past performance means seeking an understanding of the results, quality, price, and costs *as seen by the customer* to increase value to the customer and thus the value the firm provides in the marketplace. Another model describing how a firm manages its past performance is called a *maturity model* (see Chapter 4).

Regardless of the means used to analyze how a firm does or should manage its past performance, the best and highest use of past performance information is to improve performance. Subordinate uses that support this primary objective include improving feedback, improving the documentation of past performance, and improving proposals.

Improve Performance

Excellence in performance is an ongoing endeavor. It is not a static position that can be achieved and then the means of achieving it forgotten about. It is a dynamic state requiring constant improvement guided by, among other things, customer perceptions, observations, and feedback. Performance improvement efforts of merit include measures of performance to assess performance, to set direction and goals, and to measure and monitor progress. Past performance information can serve as an important component of these measures of performance.

A firm can decide by itself that it is an "excellent" performer, and this self-appraisal may even have some merit and generate strong convictions and beliefs about the value of the firm's products and services. However, in a crowded competitive field like the government contracting market, viable competitors are always present and it is not a firm's own opinion of its value that matters, but the perception, judgments, and opinions of its customers and *prospective* customers. Current customers *are already generating* past performance information about a particular firm that prospective customers will use to evaluate its past performance—while making decisions of great importance to the firm. It is toward the improvement of these perceptions and judgments that the time and energy spent managing past performance is directed. There are two elements at play here: managing and improving perceptions of performance, including the documentation of those perceptions, and using this information to improve performance itself, thus improving future perceptions of performance.

Improve Feedback

A critical element of improving performance is robust and objective feedback from a variety of sources, particularly clients, including past, current, and prospective clients. For a large number of government contractors, past performance information represents the only customer satisfaction information they receive outside of direct feedback during performance. Past performance information provided by government agencies is also a low- or no-cost means of receiving customer feedback. Active involvement and management of this information flow is an important element of obtaining actionable customer feedback on performance.

An example of how a firm can actively manage and participate in this feedback loop to improve the feedback received is to perform self-assessments before a CPARS assessment is due, since on an ongoing project, the due dates for CPARS performance assessment by the customer are known. Well in advance of this due date, the firm can take a CPARS form, prepopulate the pro forma contract and administrative blocks, and use the elements in the form to complete a self-assessment of its own performance, assigning ratings it feels are appropriate for its own performance. The next step is to schedule a time with the rating official, most likely the contracting officer's representative, to go over this self-assessment. The purpose of this session is to have a frank and open discussion regarding performance and to identify areas where the government evaluator sees a need for (or there is room for) improvement. The firm, armed with this information, can then use the remaining time between the discussion and the end of the rating period to address these areas and improve the evaluation against what it would have been had the feedback session not been held.

Improve Documentation of Past Performance

People are more inclined to act than they are to write about an action—particularly the actions of others—and documentation of past performance is essentially writing retrospectively about the actions of others. Human nature runs counter to efforts to improve documentation, as evidenced by low rates of completed CPARS reporting. Sellers in the past performance cycle must overcome this tendency in order to improve their documentation of past performance.

There are a number of means to achieve this goal, some of which include increasing the number of channels and types of feedback received, making CPARS reports more comprehensive and more complete, and increasing the posting of CPARS comments by the seller. The seller must take advantage of every opportunity to "complete the story" in a CPARS report by fully using the comments section or reminding government clients to complete CPARS reports. See Chapter 4 for specifics on how a firm can institutionalize these actions by describing them in plain language and assigning them as specific responsibilities to ensure they are accomplished.

Having an active customer satisfaction program is one way to increase the number of channels and types of feedback received. A customer satisfaction program can be tailored to elicit feedback from those that will respond to phone conversations but not to email queries, for instance. Elicitation and capture of customer quotes and awards or "attaboys" is another example of a concentrated effort to open up and encourage additional types of (positive) feedback that can be incorporated into past performance documentation. CPARS reports allow approximately one page of contractor comments and a generous allotment of 60 days in which to complete the comments. Few firms take the time to use these comment sections. Many equate the use of the comments sections to disputing the ratings received, which is neither their stated purpose nor the only way to make use of them. The comments section can be used to complete the story of each record, the story being a complete, stand-alone description of all aspects of the performance during the rating period that can then be understood by a wider audience relying upon this past performance documentation during evaluations of past performance.

Improve Proposals

We have identified improving performance as the primary objective of managing past performance. During contract performance, past performance information that will be used for bids and proposals is generated. Improved proposals generally result in more opportunities for performance. Thus we have established a self-reinforcing, positive feedback loop in which better performance results in more past performance information that, if managed well, results in improved proposals which in turn result in better performance. How past performance information can be best managed to improve proposals is covered in greater detail in Chapter 4 and Chapter 5.

Chapter 3

PAST PERFORMANCE AS STORYTELLING

- →

A government solicitation always provides specific instructions regarding the past performance information it requires from an offeror. Generally speaking, it details requirements for factual data about the offeror's past performance on a contract, including such data as the scope of services, period of performance, dollar value, type of contract, and a variety of other factors. Solicitations also allow varying degrees of flexibility in the "write-up" describing how the work an offeror has performed in the past has impacted its clients and delivered results. The best way for an offeror to showcase its past performance in write-ups is to lay out a compelling story that affirms a contractor's expertise and its commitment to a past project. This narrative will reinforce the impression given by the data that contract award to the offeror is low risk, that the offeror is reliable, and that its past performance is highly relevant to the current project.

Contractors need to adopt a methodical approach to the past performance write-up that helps them develop a compelling story about their experience and qualifications to perform at a high level for a project on which they plan to bid. We describe such an approach in this chapter. As a best practice, managing past performance information is a continuous process that begins with a contract award and carries through to documenting a firm's performance at various levels of detail in the project. It continues on to the presentation of that information—how it describes its role in the project—when it is placing offers on new solicitations. *Past performance as storytelling* means creating stories that represent an honest and thorough evaluation of the skills that a company can bring to any prospective, relevant project.

The most important consideration in creating a best-practice past performance write-up is the characteristics and nature of the evaluators, who each have their own information needs. Many people will read a write-up—the contracting officer, a government program manager, and other technical managers or specialists as needed, forming the proposal review team. The offeror must understand who they are and meet each individual's needs; it should not use cookie-cutter proposals or past performance write-ups, but should instead tailor its write-up to enhance its position as the offeror to select on a particular solicitation.

When a company creates a past performance write-up, it should follow four steps or phases to produce a story that the proposal review team can understand and, more importantly, that effectively identifies the contractor with the story in a way that clearly establishes it as the best choice for the (similar) pending project:

1. Providing just the facts
2. Providing context
3. Providing impact
4. Increasing understanding.

These steps are highly effective tools for developing a past performance write-up for an ongoing project that will become a source of past performance information for future proposals. Everyone engaged in the project should contribute to the development of the past performance write-up, and the project manager should add items as they arise. Each step performs a specific function in convincing evaluators of a firm's ability to effectively manage the project being bid on. As the story of past performance experiences is built, its message of delivering above and beyond the client's requirements should increase the evaluation team's confidence in the firm, leading to a low risk rating and possibly a positive recommendation for award.

Each level also serves a specific purpose in describing the firm's past work as it relates to a new solicitation's performance work statement (PWS).

Fictional examples provide a visual accompaniment to the discussion to aid in understanding each step as well as how an evaluation team may view the information. These exhibits present the steps as layers or dimensions that can and should be added to a company's past performance information as it is developed, from contract award through proposal development for the next offer.

PROVIDING JUST THE FACTS

The most basic past performance write-up presents a just-the-facts scenario. It is written at the time a contract is awarded or shortly thereafter. At this point, there is no specific knowledge of the actual *quality* of performance, so the write-up describes the scope and nature of the work to be performed.

This type of write-up is the starting point for ongoing past performance information development. It allows presentation of customer experience at a basic level. It is often used for a presentation of capability for potential industry partners or other relevant parties. Just-the-facts write-ups may be adequate for producing a capability statement or a response to a request for information demonstrating involvement in projects of similar size and scope. In these situations, the government review team is most interested in capability and similarity of services to its own requirements.

While this past performance write-up does an excellent job of detailing the contract data and scope of work, it does not provide much understanding of the challenges a firm faced during project execution. Consequently, the evaluator has little opportunity or detail with which to relate current requirements or circumstances with those of the past customer, which presents challenges in drawing conclusions about that firm's ability to solve the agency's problem or meet its needs.

A relevance section can be added to the past performance write-up for specific proposal opportunities or the proposal in which it is used. The relevance section is customized to the new proposal and the statement of work, PWS, or service requirements of the agency review team. If a past performance questionnaire (PPQ) is required, the degree of success and progress the execution team has made on the project should be considered before it is submitted. A PPQ for a new project could score low if the project is just under way and no real deliverables have been developed and rapport with government personnel has not been established. In this case, a different project with a real success story should be considered as a reference.

Exhibit 3-A at the end of this chapter shows an example of a "just-the-facts" past performance write-up. The entries in the upper portion represent information frequently required by instructions included in a request for proposal (RFP) and likely to appear in any past performance write-up. The work description is free-form and can be more extensive than shown in the sample. The sample addresses relevance by citing paragraphs in the PWS that are similar in scope to the past project being referenced. This could be more explicitly stated at this level, but this sample just sticks to the fact that the past and current efforts share common services in the PWS.

PROVIDING CONTEXT

In this phase, an offeror begins to customize the past performance write-up based on the proposal scope and prospective customer's needs and problems. The just-the-facts past performance write-up does not provide any depth of understanding of the challenges that a contractor has or any real issues it addresses during the course of its work for the government. These details are added as the project matures and the project staff are engaged by it, all of whom should contribute to developing the past performance write-up by adding context.

Adding context allows creation of a stronger link between contractor and project and a clearer picture of the customer's true needs, fostering a better understanding of the customer's motivation in seeking contractor support. Through this understanding, a prospective client's evaluator will see that the firm being evaluated supported another customer with comparable needs and issues. This sets the stage for the evaluator's identification with an offeror's past performance experience. Ideally, this identification will result in the offeror's proposal being assigned a lower risk.

To put a firm's past performance in context, background information about the current customer, the agency's mission, technical challenges, cost constraints, and history of issues with the specific support being requested must be incorporated. It is important to obtain a precise understanding of any *prospective* customer's issues and motivation in seeking support. That understanding presents the contractor with an opportunity to highlight similarities between past and prospective clients.

In Exhibit 3-B, a section specifically identifies the agency's requirements. This section can be used to elaborate on a variety of related matters such as the customer's mission and specific challenges or issues faced on the referenced project. There is still a description of the work performed, but a separate presentation of the customer's situation and issues is also presented. The focus of this write-up is conveying that the referenced customer had a specific need that the contractor's work satisfied. The sections providing facts on the referenced contract and its relevance to the new PWS remain the same as in the just-the-facts write-up.

SHOWING IMPACT

Every contractor wants to believe that its work had a positive impact on the customers and made a real difference for the client. Truthfully, a positive impact should occur at some point in every contract or customer interaction. However, simple customer satisfaction, by itself, is expected and will not stand out. Offerors need to show that their past performance shows more substance than just another happy client—they need to factually present the information in a way that helps the evaluation team see how the past project results relate to its own desired outcome.

When a firm evaluates its own past performance to select relevant references to include in a current proposal, it should select projects where the scope of work is similar to the current proposal. This permits the evaluation team to identify with these past projects easily. However, the impact of a past performance project does not necessarily need to relate to a problem with which the prospective client can identify. Evaluators understand that a positive benefit to past customers represents an opportunity for an offeror to provide a very different positive benefit for their organization. Hence, showing a prospective customer how the offeror delivered a beneficial outcome for past customers is viewed as a positive attribute. Proof that the offeror has such past performance history reduces the perception of risk associated with awarding a subsequent contract to that contractor.

The example past performance write-up now has an additional section called *Performance Assessment,* which allows a contractor to perform a self-assessment (Exhibit 3-C). This is an opportunity to deliver just such an impact statement: how the contractor provided some great benefit for the agency it worked with. The statement should not be dramatic but direct and factual so that the benefits are clear. At times, benefits may need to be cited in more general terms so an evaluator can relate to them, but in any case we recommend that benefits be organized into categories and labeled. This will make the list easier to read and provide tags an evaluator can use to label and refer to each benefit.

Some benefits may prove even more memorable if the evaluator has confronted issues in that area on past contracts. For example, the incumbent contractor may have failed to provide deliverables on the agreed-upon schedule. Proposal teams will not always look at timeliness as a benefit because projects should always be completed in a timely manner. However, if the offeror has earned praise for meeting or exceeding the schedule under *timeliness of performance*, that will carry special weight and will likely be favorably viewed by the evaluator. In this case, timeliness takes on increased significance because of the review team's negative experience with the incumbent contractor.

INCREASING UNDERSTANDING

So far in this series of examples, the evaluator has learned about these elements of the firm's past performance:

- Past customer's requirements
- Past customer's mission and issues
- The scope of the services provided by the contractor
- How the services benefited the customer in an impactful and meaningful way
- The relevance of that support to the requirements solicited.

Ideally, by reviewing the information provided by the offeror, the evaluator comes to understand that the offeror could perform the required work with a low risk of failure. This is the optimal outcome and a very acceptable result of the past performance write-up. But more can be done to increase evaluators' understanding that the firm's past performance directly correlates with the new project tasks.

This can be achieved by presenting compelling information in the past performance write-up. With that goal in mind, a detailed presentation of the specific accomplishments of the past project *related to each task* required under the new bid is included in the proposal. This presentation clearly articulates past success on the related tasks requirements and, combined with the other descriptions of past performance, should lead to the lowest risk rating possible.

At times, a contractor's performance record shows that something extraordinary has been accomplished. Perhaps it was an outcome that could not have been predicted and was not expected, but nevertheless it clearly shows something positive. The hope is that the accomplishment will have value for the evaluators of the proposal, who upon reading of these results see how their agency would benefit from a similar outcome with the proposed project.

In the final example (Exhibit 3-D), the past performance write-up presents details on how similar work was conducted in another environment that resulted in a positive customer outcome. By reviewing this detailed information on how the prior work was performed, the evaluator can learn how his work requirements might be approached differently to achieve a more positive outcome. Not all past performance projects have an opportunity to present this characteristic. However, when it is possible to demonstrate a similar positive customer outcome, that information may favorably influence the evaluation.

Exhibit 3-D also contains a past performance description where several elements of support services for the prior project were combined. This action resulted in cost efficiencies being achieved that permitted the prior customer to de-obligate funds against the contract and free those funds up to be used for acquiring other services within the agency. This is the kind of positive outcome that a government customer can relate to and thus view favorably in its evaluation of an offeror's past performance.

Exhibit 3-A: "Just-the-Facts" Write-Up

U.S. Agency of the Federal Government IT Systems Support Services	
Firm Performing Work	Offeror Corporation, Inc. Corporate Drive, Any City, ST 12345
Contracting Activity	USAFG Acquisition Services, Government Address, Any City, ST 12345
Technical Representative	USAFG End-User Support, Government Address, Any City, ST 12345 Contract Technical Rep, contracts.tech.rep@usafg.gov, 102-123-5678
Contract Administration	USAFG Acquisition Services, Government Address, Any City, ST 12345 Contracting Officer, contracts.officer@usafg.gov, 102-123-4567
Contract Number:	AFG001-13-C-0001
Contract Type:	T&M
Contract Value:	$ 12,345,000
Delivery Schedule:	10/1/2013- 9/30/2018

Description of Work Performed

Offeror Corporation, Inc. (Offeror) provides a range of technology support services to help the U.S. Agency of the Federal Government (USAFG) in support of its mission. Offeror provides IT infrastructure operations and engineering services to support the Chief Information Officer, ensuring that the USAFG IT enterprise is reliable and evolves to support emerging requirements. We provide infrastructure services and full lifecycle IT support to manage data network infrastructure systems and services at headquarters and field locations.

Offeror manages and maintains the USAFG infrastructure, supporting over 5,000 users across headquarters and field offices nationwide. We staff and operate a consolidated 24x7x365 help desk, responding to approximately 15,000 end-user service actions per year. Offeror provides program management, systems engineering, integration, testing, and configuration management within USAFG's IT infrastructure, including network security engineering and maintaining a VPN remote access capability. We operate a depot maintenance facility with the capability to receive, ship and store spare parts/systems; and to perform troubleshooting and repairs.

Our project management ensures consistent delivery of high-quality services. Our project management systems provide extensive SLA information — exceeding contract SLA reporting requirements. We help USAFG respond to legislative mandates and Congressional requests, and collect and analyze data for mission planning. Offeror provides a full range of data center services, data network services, end user services, service desk support and asset management.

Relevance to Work Required by PWS

This project is **very relevant** to Buyer's PWS. Offeror has performed similar work within the last **5 years** that is **very relevant** to PWS Task 1: Service Delivery Operations, Task 2: Engineering, Integration and Release Readiness, Task 3: Logistics and Asset Management, Task 4: Field Service and Depot Maintenance Support, and Task 6: Project Management.

Exhibit 3-B: Write-Up with Context Added

U.S. Agency of the Federal Government IT Systems Support Services	
Firm Performing Work	Offeror Corporation, Inc. Corporate Drive, Any City, ST 12345
Contracting Activity	USAFG Acquisition Services, Government Address, Any City, ST 12345
Technical Representative	USAFG End-User Support, Government Address, Any City, ST 12345 Contract Technical Rep, contracts.tech.rep@usafg.gov, 102-123-5678
Contract Administration	USAFG Acquisition Services, Government Address, Any City, ST 12345 Contracting Officer, contracts.officer@usafg.gov, 102-123-4567
Contract Number:	AFG001-13-C-0001
Contract Type:	T&M
Contract Value:	$ 12,345,000
Delivery Schedule:	10/1/2013- 9/30/2018

USAFG's Requirements

USAFG's Chief Information Officer (CIO) provides IT infrastructure operations and engineering services to ensure that USAFG's IT enterprise is reliable and evolves to support emerging requirements. Requirements include full lifecycle IT support to manage data network infrastructure systems and services at headquarters and field offices. The scope of work spans help desk support, preventative maintenance, remedial repair of installed systems, and replacement of components that are beyond their useful life or are not economical to repair. Contractor must manage end-user service delivery, network management, and network security functions with a 24x7x365 help desk with escalation processes.

Requirements include operations and maintenance support services for deployed systems at USAFG. Requirements include operations support, repair depot operation, preventive maintenance, functional testing, and logistical support for all IT assets. USAFG provides a depot maintenance facility for contractor to receive, ship and store spare parts/systems; and to perform troubleshooting and repairs. Offeror shall assign a dedicated on-site Program Manager to manage all aspects of USAFG's requirement delivery. Contractor must support USAFG's goal to integrate IT service functions that deliver project management, engineering, integration, repair/maintenance, end-user support and asset management to meet mission requirements.

U.S. Agency of the Federal Government IT Systems Support Services

Narrative Description of Work Performed

Offeror Corporation, Inc. (Offeror) provides a range of technology support services to help the U.S. Agency of the Federal Government (USAFG) in support of its mission. Offeror manages and maintains the USAFG infrastructure, supporting over 5,000 users across headquarters and field offices nationwide. We staff and operate a consolidated 24x7x365 help desk, responding to approximately 15,000 end-user service actions per year. Offeror provides program management, systems engineering, integration, testing, and configuration management within USAFG's IT infrastructure, including network security engineering and maintaining a VPN remote access capability.

Offeror provides IT infrastructure operations and engineering services to support the Chief Information Officer, ensuring that the USAFG IT enterprise is reliable and evolves to support emerging requirements. We provide infrastructure services and full lifecycle IT support to manage data network infrastructure systems and services at headquarters and field locations.

Our project management ensures consistent delivery of high-quality services. Our project management systems provide extensive SLA information — exceeding contract SLA reporting requirements. We help USAFG respond to legislative mandates and Congressional requests, and collect and analyze data for mission planning. Offeror provides a full range of data center services, data network services, end user services, service desk support and asset management.

Relevance to Work Required by PWS

This project is **very relevant** to Buyer's PWS. Offeror has performed similar work within the last **5 years** that is **very relevant** to PWS Task 1: Service Delivery Operations, Task 2: Engineering, Integration and Release Readiness, Task 3: Logistics and Asset Management, Task 4: Field Service and Depot Maintenance Support, and Task 6: Project Management.

Exhibit 3-C: Write-Up with Impact Added

U.S. Agency of the Federal Government IT Systems Support Services	
Firm Performing Work	Offeror Corporation, Inc. Corporate Drive, Any City, ST 12345
Contracting Activity	USAFG Acquisition Services, Government Address, Any City, ST 12345
Technical Representative	USAFG End-User Support, Government Address, Any City, ST 12345 Contract Technical Rep, contracts.tech.rep@usafg.gov, 102-123-5678
Contract Administration	USAFG Acquisition Services, Government Address, Any City, ST 12345 Contracting Officer, contracts.officer@usafg.gov, 102-123-4567
Contract Number:	AFG001-13-C-0001
Contract Type:	T&M
Contract Value:	$ 12,345,000
Delivery Schedule:	10/1/2013- 9/30/2018
USAFG's Requirements	

USAFG's Chief Information Officer (CIO) provides IT infrastructure operations and engineering services to ensure that USAFG's IT enterprise is reliable and evolves to support emerging requirements. Requirements include full lifecycle IT support to manage data network infrastructure systems and services at headquarters and field offices. The scope of work spans help desk support, preventative maintenance, remedial repair of installed systems, and replacement of components that are beyond their useful life or are not economical to repair. Contractor must manage end-user service delivery, network management, and network security functions with a 24x7x365 help desk with escalation processes.

Requirements include operations and maintenance support services for deployed systems at USAFG. Requirements include operations support, repair depot operation, preventive maintenance, functional testing, and logistical support for all IT assets. USAFG provides a depot maintenance facility for contractor to receive, ship and store spare parts/systems; and to perform troubleshooting and repairs. Offeror shall assign a dedicated on-site Program Manager to manage all aspects of USAFG's requirement delivery. Contractor must support USAFG's goal to integrate IT service functions that deliver project management, engineering, integration, repair/maintenance, end-user support and asset management to meet mission requirements.

U.S. Agency of the Federal Government IT Systems Support Services
Narrative Description of Work Performed
Offeror Corporation, Inc. (Offeror) provides a range of technology support services to help the U.S. Agency of the Federal Government (USAFG) in support of its mission. Offeror manages and maintains the USAFG infrastructure, supporting over 5,000 users across headquarters and field offices nationwide. We staff and operate a consolidated 24x7x365 help desk, responding to approximately 15,000 end-user service actions per year. Offeror provides program management, systems engineering, integration, testing, and configuration management within USAFG's IT infrastructure, including network security engineering and maintaining a VPN remote access capability. Offeror provides IT infrastructure operations and engineering services to support the Chief Information Officer, ensuring that the USAFG IT enterprise is reliable and evolves to support emerging requirements. We provide infrastructure services and full lifecycle IT support to manage data network infrastructure systems and services at headquarters and field locations. We help USAFG respond to legislative mandates and Congressional requests, and collect and analyze data for mission planning. Offeror provides a full range of data center services, data network services, end user services, service desk support and asset management.
Performance Assessment
Quality of Product or Service: We have employed our ISO certified quality program to implement a comprehensive quality assurance program for this project that prevents quality defects to the highest extent possible, and mitigates quality issues should they arise. **_Timeliness of Performance:_** All services and deliverables have been consistently completed on time. Periodic deliverables (monthly status reports, etc.) are delivered on time and accepted without revision. Service level agreements (SLAs) are reviewed monthly and have all been met during the base contract year. **_Effectiveness of Controlling Project Cost:_** During the base year, offeror identified over-staffed activities and worked with USAFG to modify the staffing levels to reduce resource level for those efforts. Additionally, we reported unused budget on a timely basis and advised USAFG regarding opportunities to redirect funds to overcome budget shortfalls in other activities. **_Customer Satisfaction:_** USAFG is extremely satisfied with Offeror's service throughout the performance of this contract. Offeror has engaged a third-party consultant to conduct customer satisfaction surveys with USAFG end-users. We have received highly positive feedback across the range of USAFG end-users for this project. Additionally, we received a very positive interim CPARS review from USAFG for this project. **_Effectiveness of Project Management:_** Our project management ensures consistent delivery of high-quality services. Our project management systems provide extensive SLA information — exceeding contract SLA reporting requirements. Our monthly status reports enabled the USAFG to redirect funds on a quarterly basis, which was utilized to overcome agency budget shortfalls.
Relevance to Work Required by PWS
This project is **very relevant** to Buyer's PWS. Offeror has performed similar work within the last **5 years** that is **very relevant** to PWS Task 1: Service Delivery Operations, Task 2: Engineering, Integration and Release Readiness, Task 3: Logistics and Asset Management, Task 4: Field Service and Depot Maintenance Support, and Task 6: Project Management.

Exhibit 3-D: Write-Up with Explanation Added

U.S. Agency of the Federal Government IT Systems Support Services			
Firm Performing Work Place of Performance	Offeror Corporation, Inc. Corporate Drive, Any City, ST 12345		
Contracting Activity	USAFG Acquisition Services, Government Address, Any City, ST 12345		
Technical Representative	USAFG End-User Support, Government Address, Any City, ST 12345 Contract Technical Rep, contracts.tech.rep@usafg.gov, 102-123-5678		
Contract Administration	USAFG Acquisition Services, Government Address, Any City, ST 12345 Contracting Officer, contracts.officer@usafg.gov, 102-123-4567		
Contract Number:	AFG001-13-C-0001	Type:	T&M
Awarded Price:	$ 12,345,000	Final Price	$ 12,345,000
Original Delivery Schedule:	10/1/2013- 9/30/2018	Final / Projected Delivery	10/1/2013— 9/30/2018

USAFG's Requirements

USAFG's Chief Information Officer (CIO) provides IT infrastructure operations and engineering services to ensure that USAFG's IT enterprise is reliable and evolves to support emerging requirements. Requirements include full lifecycle IT support to manage data network infrastructure systems and services at headquarters and field offices. The scope of work spans help desk support, preventative maintenance, remedial repair of installed systems, and replacement of components that are beyond their useful life or are not economical to repair. Constant changes in mission requirements coupled with the implementation of newly released, advanced technologies require the contractor to be flexible and adapt to changes in work requirements, personnel qualifications and delivery schedules.

Requirements include operations and maintenance support services for deployed systems at USAFG. Requirements include operations support, repair depot operation, preventive maintenance, functional testing, and logistical support for all IT assets. Contractor must support USAFG's goal to integrate IT service functions that deliver project management, engineering, integration, repair/maintenance, end-user support and asset management to meet mission requirements.

U.S. Agency of the Federal Government IT Systems Support Services
Narrative Description of Work Performed

Offeror Corporation, Inc. (Offeror) provides a range of technology support services to help the U.S. Agency of the Federal Government (USAFG) in support of its mission. Offeror manages and maintains the USAFG infrastructure, supporting over 5,000 users across headquarters and field offices nationwide. We staff and operate a consolidated 24x7x365 help desk, responding to approximately 15,000 end-user service actions per year. Offeror provides program management, systems engineering, integration, testing, and configuration management within USAFG's IT infrastructure, including network security engineering and maintaining a VPN remote access capability.

Offeror provides IT infrastructure operations and engineering services to support the Chief Information Officer, ensuring that the USAFG IT enterprise is reliable and evolves to support emerging requirements. We provide infrastructure services and full lifecycle IT support to manage data network infrastructure systems and services at headquarters and field locations. We help USAFG respond to legislative mandates and Congressional requests, and collect and analyze data for mission planning. Offeror provides a full range of data center services, data network services, end user services, service desk support and asset management.

Performance Assessment

Quality of Product or Service: We have employed our ISO certified quality program to implement a comprehensive quality assurance program for this project that prevents quality defects to the highest extent possible, and mitigates quality issues should they arise.

Timeliness of Performance: All services and deliverables have been consistently completed on time. Periodic deliverables (monthly status reports, etc.) are delivered on time and accepted without revision. Service level agreements (SLAs) are reviewed monthly and have all been met during the base contract year.

Effectiveness of Controlling Project Cost: During the base year, offeror identified over-staffed activities and worked with USAFG to modify the staffing levels to reduce resource level for those efforts. Additionally, we reported unused budget on a timely basis and advised USAFG regarding opportunities to redirect funds to overcome budget shortfalls in other activities.

Customer Satisfaction: USAFG is extremely satisfied with Offeror's service throughout the performance of this contract. Offeror has engaged a third-party consultant to conduct customer satisfaction surveys with USAFG end-users. We have received highly positive feedback across the range of USAFG end-users for this project. Additionally, we received a very positive interim CPARS review from USAFG for this project.

Effectiveness of Project Management: Our project management ensures consistent delivery of high-quality services. Our project management systems provide extensive SLA information — exceeding contract SLA reporting requirements. Our monthly status reports enabled the USAFG to redirect funds on a quarterly basis, which was utilized to overcome agency budget shortfalls.

U.S. Agency of the Federal Government IT Systems Support Services					
Relevance to Work Required by PWS					
Task 1	Task 2	Task 3	Task 4	Task 5	Task 6
✓	✓	✓	✓		✓

This project is **very relevant** to Buyer's PWS. Offeror has performed similar work within the last **5 years** that is **very relevant** to Tasks 1, 2, 3, 4 and 6.

Task 1 Service Desk Operation: Manage and operate end-user service delivery, network management, and network security functions with a consolidated help desk staffed 24x7x365. Staff and operate a three-tier help desk with integrated escalation processes. Provide uniform processes, knowledge sharing, and practices that maximize rapid, first-call resolution. Monitor call volume trends and adjust staffing levels to handle normal and surge call volumes. Proactively analyze incident trends and service desk performance metrics, and provide additional training and modify scripts.

Task 2 Engineering, Integration and Release Readiness: Offeror manages USAFG's IT infrastructure; including servers, hubs, switches and routers. We achieve 100% on all monthly SLAs. Our support includes operations for the enterprise operations center, which consist of Windows and Unix servers. It also includes database management and maintenance services, and performance tuning and interface development for enterprise databases. We engineered and deployed a Storage Area Network to provide expanded data storage capabilities that provided more effective data replication, data security, and costs effectiveness. We monitor and manage network, application, and server performance; collect performance statistics; and track system events to improve network availability to end-users.

Task 3 Logistics and Asset Management: Offeror logistic professionals maintain warranty, lifecycle management, and repair parts for all IT assets. This support includes acquiring and stocking repair/spare parts and systems required to support all enterprise systems. Our team assessed current inventory database, documentation structure, associated policies and procedures and offered recommendations for improvements in asset management operations.

Task 4 Field Service and Depot Maintenance Support: Offeror employs a fully qualified staff of technical support personnel to support this contract. Personnel selected possess past experience, training and qualifications with the enterprise environment used by USAFG. Offeror technicians are fully versed in the maintenance and repair of USAFG systems. USAFG provides space for a depot maintenance facility. This facility has the capability to receive, ship and store spare parts/systems; and to perform troubleshooting and repairs.

Task 6 Project Management: To successfully manage the dynamic demands of USAFG's enterprise IT environment while minimizing layers of management and oversight, Offeror has assigned a dedicated Program Manager to monitor and manage all aspects of USAFG's requirements. Each task has a separate SLA, staffing plan, schedule and budget. Our project manager actively monitors and manages SLA performance, schedules and budgets. In addition, we use decision trees and tools to quickly identify the proper escalation path for any issues that arise, ensuring they are addressed promptly and effectively, to the customer's satisfaction.

Chapter 4

PAST PERFORMANCE INFORMATION

--➔

What past performance information is stored? Who stores it, how do they store it, how it is accessed, and how it is managed? An organization needs to actively manage its data across the data lifecycle (e.g., acquire/create, store/distribute, use, archive/maintain, and dispose). Regardless of who owns and controls the information, obtaining maximum value from past performance information repositories requires developing, implementing, and executing policies, procedures, architectures, and technologies that support the owner's mission or role in the past performance cycle.

Although the evaluation and use of past performance information are topics covered in other chapters, it is important for past performance information managers at all levels to understand the intended (or desired) use of stored information when designing, implementing, and managing information repositories. In broad terms, there are four primary areas of consideration when implementing a repository: security concerns, the user experience, the idea of data as an asset, and the level of openness or interoperability.

Security includes where the data are physically stored (electronically or otherwise), but this is a secondary consideration and a technical topic outside the scope of this volume. It is important that the information be accessible only in a manner that does not damage a party through disclosure or allow unauthorized manipulation of historical information.

In the most useful data repositories, significant attention has been paid to the design and implementation of the *user experience*. To incorporate the user experience into the design of the repository, the designer uses what is called a *user story*. A user story conveys what a user needs or does with the repository and the information in it, stated in plain language and in the vernacular of the user. A user story specifies the functions that a system must do to satisfy a user or category of users. Common templates for a user story are *"As a <role>, I want <goal/desire>"* or *"As a <role>, I want <goal/desire> so that <benefit>"* (Cohn, 2004).

At a high level, there are two categories of user of past performance information: the government agency and the contractor. A government agency user story for a past performance repository could be "As a buyer, we want to know how companies have performed so that we make better buying decisions." A contractor user story for a past performance repository could be expressed as "As a seller, we want our performance reputation to be fairly and comprehensively represented so that current and prospective clients can see and understand the value we offer." These are high-level statements directed toward a government repository, and other more specific user stories could be derived based on the particular user or repository. These plain-language user stories are used to design or modify the system or repository, and thus the user's interactions with it, by focusing on that use from the user's perspective.

The *idea of data as an asset* means to recognize that data have both intrinsic *and* instrumental value. Data that can't be accessed freely by a potential user will decrease significantly in value. The Indiana Jones warehouse model of a trove of unused past performance information in a locked warehouse with a gatekeeper bureaucracy for a custodian is an outdated model that has been proven to offer no or extremely limited value.

The Federal Funding Accountability and Transparency Act (FFATA) of 2006 and the related website www.USAspending.gov provide an example of an *open and interoperable* data repository providing accurate and timely data that enable analytics. The intent behind FFATA was to increase federal agency spending transparency and empower ordinary citizens to hold the government accountable for spending decisions. This act requires that contract award information and information about firms contracting with government agencies be made available to the public through a single, searchable website. As the custodian of these data, the government gives users direct access, allowing them to analyze it and support their conclusions. This is an embodiment of the idea of data as an asset, since the data are maintained in a manner that allows users to access and use them in ways both seen and unforeseen by the custodians.

The "level of openness" of the repository refers to using standard or open architectures and interfaces that do not unnecessarily inhibit access and manipulation. "Open" applies equally to source code, the data, and application programming interfaces or other mediums of interaction, where use of standardized or transparent protocols enables rather than hinders or restricts access.

There are three categories of repositories: government repositories, privately maintained repositories providing fee-based access, and repositories maintained by a firm for use by the firm.

GOVERNMENT REPOSITORIES

Currently, the primary government repository is the Contractor Performance Assessment Reporting System (CPARS). CPARS data are accessible through the Past Performance Information Retrieval System (PPIRS). (How data enter into the system, the degree of use, and the utility of the information in the system are discussed in Chapter 2.) Although there are other repositories, most plans for them include rolling them into a combined system. Repositories already combined into CPARS include ACASS, CCASS, and FAPIIS. Table 4-1 provides a brief description of each of these repositories.

Past Performance Tracking System	Description	Location
CPARS	Contractor Performance Assessment Reporting System. A suite of web-enabled applications used to document contractor and grantee performance information.	www.cpars.gov
PPIRS	Past Performance Information Retrieval System. A web-enabled enterprise application that provides timely and pertinent contractor past performance information to the Department of Defense and federal acquisition community for use in making source selection decisions.	www.ppirs.gov
CCASS	Construction Contractor Appraisal Support System. A web-enabled application that supports the completion, distribution, and retrieval of construction contract performance evaluations.	DD Form 2626 www.cpars.gov
ACASS	Architect-Engineer Contract Administration Support System. A web-enabled application that supports the completion, distribution, and retrieval of architect-engineer (A-E) contract performance evaluations.	DD Form 2631 www.cpars.gov
FAPIIS	Federal Awardee Performance and Integrity Information System. A module on PPIRS that provides data on potential awardees to support award decisions.	www.ppirs.gov

Table 4-1: Federal Past Performance Information Repositories

Initiatives are under way to consolidate still other repositories and increase access to them. For example, the System for Award Management (SAM) now includes the previously separate information and functionality of the Central Contractor Registration system, the Online Representations and Certifications Application, and the Excluded Parties List System. The result of this consolidation is expected to be that more people will be able to access the underlying information and functions more efficiently, and overall use and utility will increase.

In addition to SAM, an overarching initiative run by the General Services Administration (GSA) to develop what it calls the Integrated Award Environment (IAE)[9] includes further consolidation

---

[9] See www.gsa.gov/portal/content/105036 for more information.

of federal contracting databases: SAM, FedBizOpps, the Electronic Subcontracting Reporting System, and the Federal Funding Accountability and Transparency Act Sub-award Reporting System. The IAE initiative is part of an ongoing consolidation and digitization of government procurement and related systems and information that is broader than but includes CPARS and PPIRS. The projected timeline for CPARS and PPIRS incorporation into the yet-to-be-developed IAE extends beyond 2018. Unlike the government's approach to SAM, which is a legacy system maintained over the years without a clean break, the IAE initiative will build an environment that is designed from the start to be open and user-centric using current technology and architecture.

Simultaneously, the U.S. Postal Service is leading a multi-agency Federal Cloud Credential Exchange (FCCX) pilot, which is intended to provide cloud-based identity management. Identity management is one of the functionalities the IAE seeks to include, and there has been talk of incorporating FCCX functionality into the IAE. Other systems targeted to be incorporated into the IAE that include identity management capability are three that have already been rolled into SAM—Wage Determinations On-Line, Federal Procurement Data System–Next Generation, and Catalog of Federal Domestic Assistance—and PPIRS.

Information Fields

A blank CPARS form is provided as Exhibit 4-A to this chapter. An example completed CPARS form including contractor comments is provided as Exhibit 4-B. The CPARS form is web-enabled, meaning it is filled out by logging into the system at www.cpars.gov. This form is the primary collection mechanism and includes the CPARS information fields. The information in this repository falls into several categories:

- Information about the contract
- Information about the contractor
- Identification of the government parties completing the report
- Ratings of the contractor's performance in multiple categories:

  o Technical (quality of product or service)

  o Cost control (not applicable for firm-fixed-price or fixed-price with economic price adjustment arrangements)

  o Schedule/timeliness

  o Management or business relations

  o Small business subcontracting as applicable

  o Other as applicable; e.g., late payment or nonpayment to subcontractors, trafficking violations, tax delinquency, failure to report in accordance with contract terms and conditions, defective cost or pricing data, terminations, suspension, and debarments

- Narratives about the contractor's performance
- Government recommendation concerning award given this performance assessment
- Indication of agreement by the parties to the report
- Comments from the contractor.

The free text blocks (narratives/comments) are character-limited. These limitations establish a modest amount of space for narrative text to be entered. Typical CPARs, even with all narrative/comment sections completed, print out on fewer than five pages and often closer to three. Enough room is provided to make numerous points and justify comments, but not enough to include lengthy statements of work, rebuttals, or other extraneous information.

Several additional items about the CPARS information fields are worth noting:

- The only *required* narratives are the reviewing official's comments. A CPAR can be completed without filling in any of the other narrative blocks.

- A substantially important item for the contractor community is the customer's testimony concerning an award of additional work to the company. CPARS requires the completion of this sentence by the assessing official: "Given what I know today about the Contractor's ability to execute what they promised in their proposal, I <u><xxx></u> award to them today given that I had a choice." A drop-down menu presents several choices of words, from which every contractor hopes to see "definitely would" (the highest rating) chosen.

- Contractor performance information, including that in CPARS, is considered privileged source selection information, is protected by the Privacy Act, and is not releasable under the Freedom of Information Act.

- All CPARS entries are due within 120 calendar days after the end of the assessment period (one year if contract is longer than one year or after the end of the performance period).

Roles and Permissions

Roles and permissions refers to job- or function-assigned roles with permission to perform certain operations assigned to specific roles. The CPARS user manual defines eight roles, more than are normally used in a given agency[10]:

- Focal point
- Assessing official representative
- Assessing official
- Contractor representative
- Reviewing official
- Department point of contact (POC)
- Agency POC
- Senior contractor representative.

Focal points are designated by a government activity and are responsible for the collection, distribution, and control of contractor performance evaluations for that activity. Focal points designate other users by role in the system and can register contracts in the system. Focal points can assign up to five alternatives for the focal point role. Contracts should be registered within 30 days of award and can be batch-registered by the focal point.

---

[10] www.cpars.gov/cparsfiles/pdfs/CPARS_User_Manual.pdf.

Assessing official representatives can initiate and update evaluations but do not have the authority to send evaluations to the contractor representative or to finalize an evaluation. These people are sometimes contract specialists or contracting officer representatives (CORs) and can also register individual contracts in the system.

Assessing officials are typically CORs or contracting officers and are responsible for evaluating contractor performance and for validating proposed ratings and remarks entered by assessing official representative(s). Assessing officials can forward evaluations to contractor representatives for review and comment and have the authority to close, modify, or forward the evaluation to the reviewing official. Assessing officials can modify or delete CPARs. If a CPAR is modified (e.g., evaluation ratings are changed), both the original evaluation, including comments, and the revised evaluation are visible under different tabs in the record.

The *contractor representative* is on the seller side and is responsible for reviewing and commenting on proposed ratings and remarks. Firms typically assign this role to a person in the contracts department. Contractor representatives can view individual CPARs as well as CPARS summaries and status reports.

Reviewing officials are typically contracting officers and are responsible for ensuring that the evaluation is a fair and accurate evaluation of the contractor's performance for the specific contract or order and performance period. The reviewing official must acknowledge consideration of any significant discrepancies between the assessing official's evaluation and the contractor's remarks.

The *department POC* role offers complete visibility of the CPARS process across a government department. This role is sometimes used to give access to agency POCs who require oversight of the CPARS process for specific organizations within the department.

Similarly, an *agency POC* is a senior-level employee (or designated representative) who is a proponent of the CPARS application and process. This role is intended to allow agency POCs access to the status of contracts or orders and evaluations within their agencies.

Senior contractor representatives' access allows a designated corporate official to view specific in-process and completed evaluations. This role allows a contractor functionality similar to that of the agency or department POC. The government intent behind this role is to allow the senior contractor representative to quickly identify evaluations that have been sent to the company for comment.

Aside from role-based permissions, government access to the information in PPIRS is restricted to individuals working on source selections, including contractor responsibility determinations. Contractors' access is limited to viewing their own data using a marketing partner identification number assigned in the contractor's SAM profile.

Data Retention

Past performance information may be obtained from PPIRS for use in source selection evaluations for up to three years (or six years for construction and architect-engineer contracts). PPIRS archives and takes offline past performance data three (or six) years after the data are entered into PPIRS from CPARS.

Reports

Four management reports are accessible from within CPARS: the CPAR status report, the contract status report, the rating metrics report, and the processing times report. These four reports (and sections of them) are access-limited based on the role of the user in question.[11]

The *CPAR status report* displays information as counts (e.g., number of evaluations complete) or as a list of available evaluations that provides the user read-only access to each evaluation. An activity

---

[11] Additionally, quarterly CPARS metrics are available to the public at www.cpars. gov/apps/cpars/metrics.htm.

log that is accessible within the CPAR status report shows an audit trail of the history of actions taken on the evaluation. For example, it identifies when the applicable contract or order was registered, when the evaluation was initiated, and who took the action(s).

The *contract status report* displays the status of contracts/order(s) as counts (e.g., number of contracts/orders due for evaluation), as a list of assigned users by status (e.g., current, due, overdue), or as a list of contracts/orders by status (e.g., current, due, overdue).

The *ratings metrics report* displays the distribution of ratings for all completed evaluations assigned to the user. The report can be qualified by date or organization.

The *processing times report* displays the processing times for all evaluations under the user's cognizance. For example, this report will identify the number of evaluations completed for a specific month and how many were completed within the 120-day objective.

Access to PPIRS is controlled by *group owners* or lead members of groups established for this purpose across the government. Two reports are accessible from within PPIRS: *report cards* and *statistical reporting*. PPIRS report cards provide a query capability for authorized users to retrieve information detailing a contractor's past performance. Report cards also allow retrieval of CPARS assessments.

PPIRS statistical reporting provides past delivery and quality performance information for commodities including contracts under the FAR 14.1502 thresholds in the PPIRS report card system. Previous sources of data (now phased out) include the Department of the Navy's Product Data Reporting and Evaluation Program, the Army's Logistics Modernization Program—Virtual Contracting Enterprise Reporting and Delinquency System, the Air Force's JO18 (Delivery), the Joint Deficiency Reporting System for joint services aviation product quality deficiency reports, and the Defense Logistics Agency's Enterprise Business System's eProcurement tool. Contractor delivery performance is based on a weighted combination of the percentage of contract line items with on-time deliveries and the average days late for all deliveries.[12]

Persistent issues exist with (1) agencies completing CPARs and other past performance evaluations and (2) agencies providing sufficient information in completed CPARs to make them useful. As recently as 2011, the Office of Federal Procurement Policy (OFPP) noted (2011) that fewer than half of the narrative blocks in CPARs were being completed and that CPARs lacked sufficient information to be useful to other contracting officers during source selection. In those agencies that have attempted to improve the completion level of CPARS reports, the available reports have been somewhat helpful. However, less attention has been paid to improving the *content* of reports and thus the utility of CPARs for their stated primary purpose: being used in source selection evaluations.

PRIVATE REPOSITORIES

Private repositories of past performance information are not typically used by more than one firm. Firms that have the scale of operations to support using some form of supplier rating scheme typically have a system tailored to their own unique needs and competencies. Service providers of supplier management systems and supply chain management software offer marketplaces or exchanges in which business transactions can be conducted, and a part of these marketplaces is the ability to rate transactions and parties (buyers and sellers) involved in transactions. The government's past performance repository system is a closer kin of a single-firm system of supplier rating tailored to one buyer. The only firm that has a dominant market position in supplier rating that is not specific to a particular buyer is Dun & Bradstreet's Open Ratings, Inc., used by the government

---

[12] The formula and weights for delivery performance are: Delivery Score = (On-time Weight × On-time Score) + (Average Days Late Weight × Average Days Late Score). Contractor quality performance by Federal Supply Code (FSC) is also formula based and equal to: (Positive weighted data − negative weighted data) / Contract FSC Line Item Total).

in some procurements, notably in solicitations for federal supply schedules.

Open Ratings is positioned as a neutral, third-party rating service. It started up in 2000 and was acquired by Dun & Bradstreet in 2006. Open Ratings is used by institutional buyers as well as the government and offers a means to assess supplier past performance. Dun & Bradstreet has a much longer history and established brand offering business information services, including supplier ratings of creditworthiness. Creditworthiness ratings are based on financial performance against industry benchmarks in the areas of payment performance, credit scoring, and financial stress scoring, which are combined into an overall composite credit appraisal. A separate rating scheme and models are used for smaller businesses with benchmarks against a separate pool of like-sized businesses. The frequency of usage of these credit-oriented assessments and ratings varies between government agencies.

The solicitation language specific to Open Ratings in use by GSA as of October 2014 states, in part:

> (ii) Factor Two—Past Performance: The Offeror must order and obtain a Past Performance Evaluation from Open Ratings, Inc. (ORI). Offerors are responsible for payment to ORI for the Past Performance Evaluation.
>
> (A) Past Performance Evaluations are valid for a period of one year from the date of issuance by ORI. If the evaluation was issued more than one year prior to the date of proposal submission via eOffer, the proposal will be rejected.
>
> (B) The order form must be completed with a minimum of six (6) customer references submitted. A "customer reference" is defined as a person or company that has purchased relevant products/services from the Offeror. The Offeror is advised to use references from projects involving products/services related to this solicitation and/or those performed under NAICS code(s) applicable to proposed products/services.
>
> (C) The Offeror must submit one (1) copy of the completed Past Performance Evaluation and one (1) copy of the order form with

its proposal. Failure to submit the completed evaluation and order form will result in rejection of the proposal.

(D) The Offeror must address any negative feedback for each of the feedback categories contained in the ORI report, to include actions taken to minimize the problems that resulted in negative feedback. (GSA, 2014: vii)

Information Fields

The respondents to an Open Ratings survey complete an online survey form. This form is the primary data collection mechanism. Open Ratings will not complete a report unless a minimum of four parties respond to the survey. The information in this repository is organized into four categories:

1. Information about the company
2. Performance ratings
3. Distribution of survey feedback from past customers
4. Information about the customer references who were surveyed.

Open Ratings survey respondents' main effort is to rate the company in question on ten factors:

1. Reliability
2. Cost
3. Order accuracy
4. Delivery/timeliness
5. Quality
6. Business relations
7. Personnel
8. Customer support
9. Responsiveness
10. Overall performance.

Survey respondents are required to provide ratings for all ten factors; however, they have the option of choosing "N/A" ("not applicable"). There is one optional free text field under the "general comments" section (the instructions read "Feel free to add any additional comments regarding your experience"), but currently these data do not appear on the final report.

In the report, a distribution of feedback scores is provided. It that shows a bar graph/percentage breakdown of responses received in the ten factor areas, detailing the percentage of respondents assigned positive, neutral, or negative scores.

Roles and Permissions

Three roles regarding Open Ratings past performance evaluations are worthy of mention: the report recipient's role, the respondent's role, and Open Ratings' role. The report recipient receives the past performance evaluation report and includes the firm reported on as well as government buyers. The respondent provides descriptive input and has access for a limited period. Open Ratings' role is as steward of the data in the repository and preparer of the past performance evaluation reports.

Data Retention

When a firm purchases an evaluation from Open Ratings, the purchase price (approximately $200) includes reports sent to two designated recipients. The reports are valid for 12 months. The information collected is used for up to a year in two publicly acknowledged ways: (1) when preparing performance evaluation reports comparing firms with the same standard industrial classification code and (2) in preparing past performance evaluations of the firm for which the information was collected.[13]

Reports

Only one report is associated with Open Ratings as a past performance evaluation tool, the past performance evaluation report shown in Exhibit 4-C.

---

[13] Interview with Dun & Bradstreet principals.

FIRM REPOSITORIES

Firms need to organize and manage their own past performance information. Considering what gets stored and how it gets stored and ensuring that it is readily accessible enables high performance in writing proposals, creating marketing campaigns, performing public relations, and carrying out performance improvement. But all too often, this function is an afterthought or a low-priority item performed by the newest hire in the business development office.

Information management requires planning to make it work smoothly; laying out and managing firm repositories does not benefit from either excessive complication or excessive control. A useful past performance repository is not a static collection of artifacts, nor is its sole value found in keeping all data in one place under lock and key. Rather, the highest value is obtained from a comprehensive, intuitively organized collection that allows and captures ideas and articulations of performance and that is a connection point for collaboration, value propositions, and creativity in expression and use. Exhibit 4-D provides a maturity model depiction of past performance information management that illuminates these and the following concepts.

The Firm's Past Performance Information Collection

A typical firm's past performance information repository begins with a handful of past performance write-ups generated while writing proposals. It is not unusual for such a fledgling repository to be non-centrally maintained or to contain duplicates (or worse, near-duplicates) for a given project. Keeping the collection of write-ups simple, quick, and intuitive is the key to moving from a disorganized mess to a user-friendly repository that does not require asking the "company expert" to hunt it down every time a specific write-up is needed. It is also important to understand and acknowledge that these write-ups are tailored for varied uses, so that there will never be just one write-up for any given project.

There are three logical first steps to assembling and organizing a past performance repository from this beginning state: (1) establishing a "production line" to pull past performance write-ups from all submitted proposals, (2) putting all the write-ups in the same place, and (3) using standard naming conventions for each write-up. One effective method at this stage is the "file-pile": Establish an electronic collection point where generators of write-ups (usually in the form of submitted proposals) do nothing more than put a copy of any documents that contain past performance write-ups. On a recurring basis, go through the pile and pull out the past performance write-ups, name the extracted write-up files using a standard, self-explanatory naming scheme and put them in the repository, whether on a shared drive or SharePoint or another multiple-access site like Google Docs. The naming scheme should be such that looking at a list of the write-up titles (or file names) is akin to looking at a table of contents that indicates the project the proposal was created for, when it was created, and perhaps the focus of the write-up. While it is tempting to include other data (e.g., the author of the write-up), requiring these additional pieces of information will stymie the effort if the "file-pile emptier" is not readily able to determine that information. The names of the write-up author or project lead, however, are very important to capture and can be captured in the metadata associated with the write-ups or in a read-me document stored with the write-ups. Tailoring the write-up will become a recurring event, and the cycle time for this work, combined with the rate of change in personnel and the multiplicity of projects in a firm, makes being able to reach out to a person familiar with the project being written about all the more critical.

Managing Past Performance Write-ups and Other Past Performance Information

Centrally storing this collection makes it more readily available but adds little value to the information. Expanding what is included in the collection (e.g., include past performance write-ups, CPARs, other customer satisfaction or feedback artifacts) is important, but merely foundational. The next step in past performance management is increasing the accessibility and content—and thus the utility and value—of the information.

Where once it was the norm to start off with some form of spreadsheet-and-shared-drive management system, the widespread use of more sophisticated collaboration or content management platforms (e.g.,SharePoint, Privia, Google Drive, or Google Docs[14]) means firms are leapfrogging past this stage. These collaborative systems, if their functionality is fully taken advantage of, can accelerate development of a past performance repository with metatagging, search capability, data structuring, version control, and activity logging.

One pitfall in centralizing is to implement over-controlling and self-limiting protocols or business rules in the collaborative software environment. Examples of this self-limiting behavior include unnecessarily limiting access to content or to user-driven interface capabilities or not recognizing and acting on the fact that the best of these platforms operate in a user-driven manner, without the need for extensive training or other people standing between the user and the content.

Moving past how and where the content is stored and how users (think every member of the team, not a select designated group) interact with it to improving the content—and your firm's *use* of the content—is to work toward a highly optimized past performance information repository.

Developing a Standard System for Past Performance Information

Standardization of data in a past performance information repository affords an opportunity to expand those data to include higher-value information. Data entered without concern for capturing standard data or metadata ensures the data will not be interoperable, making analysis almost impossible and limiting the utility of the repository. Data structures need to accommodate both free-form entries and specific completely standardized entries. A search capability is not only extremely helpful in a repository but critical and should include

---

[14] A sample compilation can be found at en.wikipedia.org/wiki/List_of_collaborative_ software.

metadata and standardized data fields as well as the free text portions of the repository (e.g., a past performance write-up or the comment blocks of a CPARS report).

Data to consider for inclusion in a company past performance repository include:

- Who performed the work on the project
- Who managed the project
- Who was the primary author of the write-up
- Awards received by performers on the project or awarded to the project or program
- Challenges and actions taken in response to them
- Tools and methods used, some very specific (e.g., Monte Carlo simulation using software "X") and some less so (e.g., company methodology for risk assessment or service delivery)
- Outcomes, both quantifiable (e.g., "saved X dollars") and subjective (reduced congressional oversight and external auditor scrutiny)
- Cost and cost performance against budget
- Schedule and any changes to schedule
- Performance
- Contract role (prime or subcontractor to a named prime)
- Contract information (competitive award, sole source, etc.)
- Contract type
- Dollar value
- Time-phased budget and total cost.

Internal Contributions to CPARS Responses and Past Performance Write-ups

As stated above, a static repository of past performance information is not the best and highest use of these data. Firms should capture performance information from internal sources as well as from clients, because developing a repository that is integral to coordination of a firm's CPARS and other customer satisfaction feedback facilitates its influence and leadership in the development of past performance information by the firm itself as well as by others. (See Exhibit 4-E for a sample company CPARS protocol.) In this manner, the firm can take ownership of its own past performance information. The use of the words "influence" and "leadership" here are not meant to suggest that a firm's goal should be to manipulate customers and their feedback; rather, that a firm should take proactive steps to ensure that CPARS and other customer satisfaction or performance evaluation methods include high ratings of the firm's contract performance, that clients complete CPARs or other reports for the firm at all appropriate times, and that the firm takes full advantage of all opportunities to comment on all performance evaluations.

The purpose of commenting is not to dispute (although comments could be used in part as a rebuttal) but rather to provide amplifying information of the sort typically omitted from client responses. This includes, but is not limited to, challenges overcome; performance against cost, schedule, and performance criteria; and awards or recognition received by the client or firm based upon performance during the rated period. When firms explain any negatives regarding past performance, they must use fact, logic, and sound reasoning; blame and finger pointing are not received favorably and reflect poorly on the offeror. The objective is to have each CPARS or other performance report become a stand-alone document that testifies to the superlative performance of the firm and that is written so that a third party can understand the value that the company provided and is capable of providing elsewhere.

What, one may rightfully ask, does this have to do with either internal contributions or increasing the usefulness of a past performance information repository? Plenty. First, who is observing and commenting on or evaluating project performance? "The client" or "the client's opinion is the only one that matters" are two possible answers. But consider another interested party—the firm itself and the people in it. Observations of our performance by others are important, but so are our observations of our own performance. Clients may be significantly less focused on and attentive to the details of our performance than we are; indeed, savvy clients focus on outcomes and leave the details to the contract performers. Clients busy "fighting fires" are distracted and are unlikely to be spending thoughtful or meaningful time and energy analyzing performance and writing evaluations. These not-unusual circumstances leave the performers as the most conscious of what worked, what didn't, how the performance impacted the outcome, and so on. In some cases, political or other considerations trump meaningful and substantive performance feedback. See any commentary (highlighted elsewhere in this book) on the government's lack of efficacy in documenting and collecting past performance information if this is in doubt.

Firms' past performance repository managers need to consider these realities and have mechanisms in place to capture performance information from sources and circumstances other than current and former clients. Collecting information from internal sources is an excellent example. Consider an internal awards program, where managers of projects have an opportunity to put forth and defend why their team or project is deserving of an award. Contrast the result with the input typically generated when a proposal manager sits a project lead down in front of a blank piece of paper to write up a project: The stories of challenges overcome, teamwork, and successful outcomes large and small generated by a passionate project lead promoting his or her team for a competitive (and meaningful) award will put those results to shame.

One cautionary note regarding client performance evaluations, particularly under the constrained communication channels frequently encountered in the CPARS past performance cycle, is that it is possible to encounter wicked learning (i.e., circumstances where one can mislearn) because a contractor can't know for sure why it has succeeded or failed based on an evaluation in CPARS (Wheeler, 2013; Hogarth, 2001). This is another reason why self- and internal reflection and performance evaluation are important for contractors: Although one can't control others' expressed opinions, one can learn from those opinions as well as collaborate and share with evaluators and clients.

Another item to note is that in addition to the importance of learning, documenting, and improving performance, the protection of self-interest is expected and accommodated, particularly in government systems for the collection, evaluation, and use of past performance information. For example, the CPARS report completion process includes and encourages contractors to interact with evaluators by commenting on and even seeking changes to how their past performance is evaluated and documented. Contractors should take advantage of these opportunities. Government agents should treat contractor performance evaluations as a collaborative exchange and not as an obligation for them to issue a take-it-or-leave-it expression of judgment issued without benefit of discussion.

Exhibit 4-A: Blank CPARS Report

CPARS/ACASS/CCASS/FAPIIS	Page 1 of 3

FOR OFFICIAL USE ONLY / SOURCE SELECTION INFORMATION - SEE FAR 2.101, 3.104, AND 42.1503

CONTRACTOR PERFORMANCE ASSESSMENT REPORT (CPAR) INCOMPLETE-RATED	NONSYSTEMS

1. **Name/Address of Contractor *(Division)*:** Company Name:
Division Name:
Street Address:
City, State, Zip Code:
Province/Country:
CAGE Code: DUNS+4 Number:
PSC: NAICS Code:
2. **Report Type:**
   __Interim   __Final Report   __Addendum
3. **Period of Performance Being Assessed:**
4a. **Contract Number:**   4b. **Business Sector & Sub-Sector:**

5. **Contracting Office:**
6. **Location of Contract Performance:**

7a. **Contracting Officer:**

7b. **Phone Number:**
8a. **Contract Award Date:** 8b. **Contract Effective Date:** 9. **Contract Completion Date:**

11. **Awarded Dollar Value: $**   12. **Current Contract Dollar Value: $**
13. __Competitive   __Non-Competitive
14. **Contract Type:**   FFP   FPI   FPR   CPFF   CPIF   CPAF   OTHER

15. **Key Subcontractors and Effort Performed:**
         CAGE:
         CAGE:
         CAGE:
16. **Program Title:**

17. **Contract Effort Description:**

Small Business Utilization
Does this contract include a subcontracting plan?
Date of last Individual Subcontracting Report (ISR) / Summary Subcontracting Report (SSR):

FOR OFFICIAL USE ONLY

CPARS/ACASS/CCASS/FAPIIS   Page 2 of 3

FOR OFFICIAL USE ONLY / SOURCE SELECTION INFORMATION - SEE FAR 2.101,
3.104, AND 42.1503

18. Evaluate the following Areas: Past Rating   Rating   Trend

a. Quality of Product or Service

b. Schedule

c. Cost Control

d. Business Relations

e. Management of Key Personnel

f. Utilization of Small Business

g. Other Areas:

(1):

(2):

(3):

(4):

(5):

(6):

(7):

(8):

19. N/A

20. Assessing Official Narrative:
(i.e., PMS, PMA, or Equivalent Individual) Responsible for Program, Project, or Task/
Job Order Execution

QUALITY OF PRODUCT OR SERVICE:

SCHEDULE:

COST CONTROL:

BUSINESS RELATIONS:

FOR OFFICIAL USE ONLY

CPARS/ACASS/CCASS/FAPIIS   Page 3 of 3

FOR OFFICIAL USE ONLY / SOURCE SELECTION INFORMATION - SEE FAR 2.101,
3.104, AND 42.1503

MANAGEMENT OF KEY PERSONNEL:

ADDITIONAL/OTHER:

RECOMMENDATION:

Name and Title of Assessing Official
Name:
Title: Organization:
Phone Number: Fax Number:
Email Address: Date:
Contractor Comments:

21. Name and Title of Contractor Representative
Name:
Title:
Phone Number: Fax Number:
Email Address: Date:
Review by Reviewing Official:

22. Name and Title of Reviewing Official
Name:
Title: Organization:
Phone Number: Fax Number:
Email Address: Date:

FOR OFFICIAL USE ONLY

Exhibit 4-B: Completed CPARS Report

CPARS/ACASS/CCASS/FAPIIS	Page 1 of 4

FOR OFFICIAL USE ONLY / SOURCE SELECTION INFORMATION - SEE FAR 2.101, 3.104, AND 42.1503

CONTRACTOR PERFORMANCE ASSESSMENT REPORT (CPAR) INCOMPLETE-RATED	NONSYSTEMS

1. **Name/Address of Contractor *(Division):*** Company Name: Offeror Corporation, Inc.
Division Name:
Street Address: Corporate Drive
City, State, Zip Code: Any City, ST 12345
Province/Country: US
CAGE Code: 1A123   DUNS+4 Number: 123456
PSC: A123   NAICS Code: 541519
2. **Report Type:**
  _X_Interim   __Final Report   __Addendum
3. **Period of Performance Being Assessed: 10/01/2013 to 09/30/2014**
4a. **Contract Number:**   4b. **Business Sector & Sub-Sector:**
  AGF01-13-C-0001   IT Support Services
5. **Contracting Office:**
6. **Location of Contract Performance:**

7a. **Contracting Officer:** FGA Acquisition Services
7b. **Phone Number:**
8a. **Contract Award Date: 8b. Contract Effective Date: 9. Contract Completion Date:**
09/01/2013   10/01/2013   09/30/2018
11. **Awarded Dollar Value:** $ 12,345,000   12.   **Current Contract Dollar Value:** $ 12,345,000
13. __Competitive   __Non-Competitive
14. **Contract Type:**   FFP   FPI   FPR   CPFF   CPIF   CPAF   OTHER
          Time and Material
15. **Key Subcontractors and Effort Performed:**
CAGE: CAGE: CAGE:
16. **Program Title:**
IT Systems Support Services
17. **Contract Effort Description:**
Offeror maintains the USAFG infrastructure, supporting over 5,000 end-users in Agency headquarters and field locations. They provide service delivery through a 24x7x365 Help Desk, generating roughly 15,000 service requests per year. Offeror provides engineering, testing, and release readiness for USAFG's IT infrastructure, including designing and maintaining VPN remote access.

Small Business Utilization
Does this contract include a subcontracting plan?   NO
Date of last Individual Subcontracting Report (ISR) / Summary Subcontracting Report (SSR):

FOR OFFICIAL USE ONLY

CPARS/ACASS/CCASS/FAPIIS			Page 2 of 4

FOR OFFICIAL USE ONLY / SOURCE SELECTION INFORMATION - SEE FAR 2.101, 3.104, AND 42.1503

18. Evaluate the following Areas:	Past Rating	Rating	Trend
a. Quality of Product or Service	N/A	Exceptional	N/A
b. Schedule	N/A	Unsatisfactory	N/A
c. Cost Control	N/A	Very Good	N/A
d. Business Relations	N/A	Exceptional	N/A
e. Management of Key Personnel	N/A	Satisfactory	N/A
f. Utilization of Small Business	N/A	N/A	N/A
g. Other Areas:			
(1): Program Management		Very Good	
(2):		N/A	
(3):		N/A	
(4):		N/A	
(5):		N/A	
(6):		N/A	
(7):		N/A	
(8):		N/A	

19. N/A

20. Assessing Official Narrative:
(i.e., PMS, PMA, or Equivalent Individual) Responsible for Program, Project, or Task/Job Order Execution

QUALITY OF PRODUCT OR SERVICE:
The quality of service provided by Offeror met all contract requirements. Offeror satisfied all the specifics qualifications required for personnel on the contract. Offeror provided a highly qualified team of technical experts in all the areas necessary to successful complete PWS tasks and deliver the highest level of quality to Agency.

SCHEDULE:
Most support services provided under this contract were delivered as required by USAFG's PWS. During the base period, some deliverables were delayed due to transition issues. Once the transition was completed, deliverables have been provided as agreed.

COST CONTROL:
Offeror provided savings to the USAFG as they began performance of the contract by hiring local personnel to support selected field offices which resulted in lower labor rates than originally proposed. Travel cost were also reduced base on using local staff. These revisions resulted to an overall savings of 5% for the base and option periods.

BUSINESS RELATIONS:
The interaction and working relationship with the USAFG is very good. Offeror worked well with both USAFG personnel and other contracted support personnel. USAFG is able to contact Offeror's Program Manager when needed. Offeror's PM has been responsive to USAFG's concerns. Offeror's executives make regular visits to USAFG leadership to ensure that all obligations are met and that customer satisfaction is monitored and high performance standards maintained.

MANAGEMENT OF KEY PERSONNEL:
Offeror is providing exceptional key personnel for this contract and ensures that they are continuously trained in the latest technologies and tools to deliver on the requirements of the PWS.

ADDITIONAL/OTHER:

RECOMMENDATION:

Given what I know today about the Contractor's ability to execute what they promised in their proposal, I definitely would award to them today given that I had a choice.

21 Name and Title of Assessing Official
Name: USAFG Contracting Officer
Title: Government Contracts Officer   Organization: USAFG Acquisition Services
Phone Number: 102-123-4567   Fax Number:
Email Address: contracts.officer@USAFG.gov   Date: 11/12/2014
22 Contractor Comments:

Quality:
Offeror understands the dynamic and demanding nature of USAFG's mission. Offeror, an ISO 9001:2008 certified company, strives to retain the most skilled and appropriately experienced SMEs to meet the government's requirements. Our support for USAFG's requirements is based upon our knowledge of and experience supporting five USAFG contracts as the Prime, and four USAFG contracts as a Subcontractor. Offeror is committed to providing USAFG with the highest quality personnel and to being a valuable member of the USAFG support team.

Schedule:
Following the difficulties of transition, all deliverables have been submitted on time and accepted as submitted without requiring modification. As noted, the incumbent contractor failed to provide the needed transition of deliverables in a timely fashion resulting in our delay in providing those to USAFG.

Cost Control
As stated, Offeror provided local personnel with the proven experience and tested skills necessary to support the PWS requirements resulting in a cost savings to the USAFG. Offeror strives to provide the best value to our customers and offer savings that result from effective delivery.

CPARS/ACASS/CCASS/FAPIIS   Page 4 of 4

FOR OFFICIAL USE ONLY / SOURCE SELECTION INFORMATION - SEE FAR 2.101, 3.104, AND 42.1503

Business Relations:
Offeror believes that open communication is a key to a positive working relationship. We communicate regularly through face-face discussion, or by phone and internet; and in writing via monthly reports. We inform USAFG stakeholders of matters that affect their mission and work with USAFG personnel as a partner.

Management of Key Personnel
Offeror's President oversees support to our USAFG work to ensure that we provide exceptional support for USAFG's mission. Our program management team's experience demonstrates our commitment, capability and experience in delivering reliable, effective support to USAFG's requirements.

Other Areas:
To lead this project, Offeror assigned a senior manager with extensive experience and subject matter expertise. The mission of USAFG dictates this high level of expertise and we have been responsive to their mission needs.

23. Name and Title of Contractor Representative
Name: Offeror Contracts Manager
Title: Director of Contracts
Phone Number: 202-123-4567   Fax Number:
Email Address: offeror.contracts@offeror.com   Date: 12/02/2014

24. Review by Reviewing Official:

25. Name and Title of Reviewing Official
Name:
Title: Organization:
Phone Number: Fax Number:
Email Address: Date:

FOR OFFICIAL USE ONLY

Exhibit 4-C: Example Dun & Bradstreet Open Ratings Report

Open Ratings

Past Performance Evaluation

1. COMPANY OVERVIEW

		Past Performance Evaluation	
Primary Name :	GORMAN MANUFACTURING COMPANY, INC.	Report Date:	10-18-2011
Alternate Name :	(none)	Order Number	3276213
D-U-N-S® :	80-473-5132		
Address :	492 Koller Street		
	Scan Francisco, CA 94110		
Telephone	+1 (650) 555-0000		
Number :			

Company Information	
Year Started:	1985
Year of Current Control:	1985
Annual Sales:	$ 21,665,429
Total Employees:	130
SIC/Line of Business:	2752/Commercial printing, lithographic

2. SUPPLIER PERFORMANCE RATINGS

The supplier's overall performance rating is an assessment of predicted performance. Ratings are on a scale from 0 to 100, where 100 represents the highest level of customer satisfaction. The SIC-level benchmark indicates how the supplier's overall performance rating ranks in comparison against peers.

Overall Performance Rating   79   ○○○○○

Overall, how satisfied do you feel about the performance of this company during this transaction?

SIC/Quintile

Bottom ⬜⬜⬜⬜⬜ Top

SIC: 2752/Commercial printing, lithographic

Detailed Performance Ratings

		0	25	50	75	100

RELIABILITY:
How reliably do you think this company follows through on its commitments?   79

COST:
How closely did your final total costs correspond to your expectations at the beginning of the transaction?   79

ORDER ACCURACY:
How well do you think the product/service delivered matched your order specifications and quantity?   78

DELIVERY/TIMELINESS:
How satisfied do you feel about the timeliness of the product/service delivery?   78

QUALITY:
How satisfied do you feel about the quality of the product/service provided by this company?   82

BUSINESS RELATIONS:
How easy do you think this company is to do business with?   79

PERSONNEL:
How satisfied do you feel about the attitude, courtesy, and professionalism of this company's staff?   72

CUSTOMER SUPPORT:
How satisfied do you feel about the customer support you received from this company?   77

RESPONSIVENESS:
How responsive do you think this company was to information requests, issues, or problems that arose in the course of the transaction?   78

Open Ratings

Past Performance Evaluation

Business Name : GORMAN MANUFACTURING COMPANY, INC.
D-U-N-S® : 80-473-5132
Report Date : 10-18-2011

3. DISTRIBUTION OF FEEDBACK

This supplier's ratings were based in part on survey feedback from past customers. This chart provides a breakdown of the survey responses received from customers in the last 12 months. For each of the survey questions, the responses, which were provided on a 0 to 10 scale, are categorized as "positive" (9 to 10), "neutral" (5 to 8), or "negative" (0 to 4). The percentages of responses falling into each category are shown below.

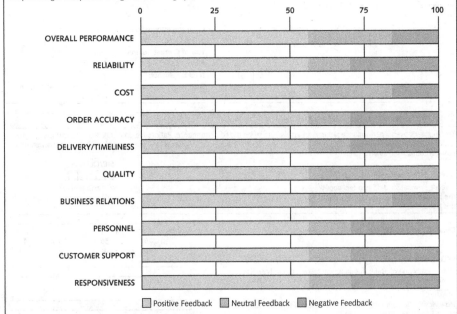

4. CUSTOMER REFERENCES SURVEYED

The most recent feedback obtained on this supplier came from companies in the following industries.
SIC/Line of Business:
   2911/Petroleum refining
   3724/Aircraft engines and engine parts
   3353/Aluminum sheet, plate, and foil
Number of surveys completed during the past 30 days is 4.

Note: The supplier ratings set forth above incorporate the responses and performance opinions of the surveyed customer references and not those of Dun & Bradstreet. Some references may not have provided ratings for all performance aspects.

The report may not be reproduced in whole or part in any manner whatsoever.

Exhibit 4-D: Past Performance Management Maturity Model

The past performance maturity model is a benchmark for measuring the maturity of an organization's past performance–related processes. This model provides a framework for prioritizing actions and a way to define what improvement means for your firm in the area of past performance processes. As shown in the model, *less mature* means less attention is paid to the collection, storage, and content of past performance write-ups and information. At higher maturity levels, there is less reliance on individual heroics to capture past performance information and more focus on actual performance improvement.

More

Maturity

Less

Optimizing
- Innovation – PP collected & used to improve performance in new ways
- Transformation – PP information use contributes to building/transforming firm and firm performance

Managed
- Quantitative process management capable
- Enterprise influence by high performance teams
- Established quality criteria
- User-driven infrastructure management
- Primary M.O. is managing relationships with users/customers of PP info

Defined
- Primary M.O. shifted to process & solution development
- Quality management applied to processes
- Organizational competency development
- Processes defined and used
- Support systems in place to manage PP content

Repeatable
- Management visibility only of finished write ups
- Primary M.O. – reactive
- Training focus is on individual skills – "replicating heroes"
- Administrative management of PP repository only

Initial
- Ad hoc/chaotic generation, retention and use of PP write ups
- No quality standards, results not repeatable
- Individual heroics required to achieve success; e.g. proposal writers create PP write-ups practically from scratch for proposal
- No or extremely little management visibility into process or write-ups

Exhibit 4-E: Sample Company CPARS Response Protocol

Purpose:

The purpose of this protocol is to describe how Company manages Contractor Performance Assessment Reporting System (CPARS) documents and responses.

Goals:

Company goals regarding CPARS are to ensure that:

- Recorded entries include high ratings of Company's contract performance
- Government Officials complete CPARS reports for Company at all appropriate times
- Company takes full advantage of all opportunities to enter comments on all filed CPARS reports

How Company Manages CPARS:

The Company Contracts Manager maintains Company CPARS login information and routinely checks for posted reports, ensuring that; accounts remain active, notifications of filed reports and actions due are distributed to the appropriate parties for action, and Company responses are filed in a timely manner.

The Company Proposal Manager manages Company responses to CPARS reports. Company responses follow two general pathways:

Concurrence with CPARS ratings and report.

In the case of CPARS reports not being disputed by Company, the standard Company response is to complete the comments section of the report. This section shall be used to provide additional amplifying information typically omitted from Government responses. This includes but is not limited to: amplifying information about challenges overcome, performance against cost, schedule and performance criteria, awards or recognition received by the client or by Company based upon Company performance during the rated period. The objective is to have each CPARS report become a stand-alone document that testifies to the superlative performance of Company and is written in a way that others besides the client writing the report can understand the value that Company provided and is capable of providing elsewhere.

Dispute CPARS ratings and report.

In the case of CPARS ratings and reports that Company disputes, the standard Company response is to engage in a direct dialogue with the rater and/or the contracting officer to revise the ratings or remarks. The ideal scenario being that the rater or contracting officer revises the ratings/remarks. Regardless of the outcome of this appeal, Company will submit comments on the CPARS report. In cases where the ratings or remarks are not favorable, extra emphasis will be placed on portraying the true circumstances that led to the reduced ratings/remarks without inclusion of inflammatory or blame-casting comments.

Additionally, the Company Proposal Manager maintains a library with a master listing of CPARS reports in the Business Development section of the Company portal.

The Company Proposal Manager arranges for reviews of CPARS comments prior to submission. Reviewers include but are not limited to Business Unit/Delivery, Business Development and Marketing leadership.

Company Program Managers maintain cognizance of the status of CPARS reports on contracts they are managing. Program Managers should understand when reports can be filed, when they are required to be filed, and when they are filed. Program Managers play an active role in raising awareness of Government Officials to ensure that reports are filed and reflect the high caliber of service provided by Company. Program Managers initiate actions by the team and Proposal Manager to pre-populate forms with contract and performance information and facilitate the timely and accurate submission of CPARS reports.

Chapter 5

PAST PERFORMANCE EVALUATIONS

---------------------------------→

Past performance evaluation is the sum of many parts. It involves more than a score on a single evaluation criterion. There are multiple perceptions, viewpoints, and methods used that all affect what information is considered, how it is considered, and how a firm's past performance is rated. Savvy firms continuously monitor and manage their past performance information and evaluations. More than that, they have a strong understanding of how to use their own past performance information to present their full capabilities and past performance records in a memorable and distinct way.

Past performance information is evaluated by the government as part of responsibility determinations, as part of source selection evaluations, and as a part of monitoring contractor performance. Although the focus here is on the federal government as the evaluator of a firm's past performance, its evaluations impact how a company will be considered when evaluated by potential business partners, financial institutions, employees, and investors as they make decisions, including contract award decisions.

RESPONSIBILITY DETERMINATION

The use of past performance in responsibility determinations (see Chapter 2) is an important element in understanding past performance evaluation. Before any government agency can award business to a firm, it must make an affirmative determination that the firm is an acceptable contractor. In other words—the firm must be deemed *responsible* for the project.

FAR 9.1 and associated provisions of the United States Code consider a *responsible* contractor to have the capability, tenacity, and perseverance to perform. These laws require agencies to make awards only to responsible contractors. The FAR lists the general standards that a contractor must meet to be considered responsible, which include the following:

1. Have adequate financial resources to perform the contract or the ability to obtain them

2. Be able to comply with the required or proposed delivery or performance schedule, taking into consideration all existing commercial and governmental business commitments

3. Have a satisfactory performance record

4. Have a satisfactory record of integrity and business ethics

5. Have the necessary organization, experience, accounting and operational controls, and technical skills or the ability to obtain them

6. Have the necessary production, construction, and technical equipment and facilities or the ability to obtain them

7. Be otherwise qualified and eligible to receive an award under applicable laws and regulations.

CONTRACTOR PERFORMANCE MONITORING

Government agencies use performance information collected during the monitoring of a contractor's current performance as part of their future source selection evaluations. Under the normal process of responding to a government solicitation, contractors will have time to carefully craft and shape the past performance components (e.g., past performance write-up, proof points, narrative segments) in a proposal submission. But contractors do not have the direct ability to shape past performance information collected during contract performance, particularly the CPARS comment blocks, which are closer in form and content to a past performance questionnaire than to a past performance write-up. This makes it critical that a firm takes the time throughout the collection and response cycle during contract performance, such as is done with CPARs, to add comments even to glowing appraisals, rounding out the story of the great work accomplished by the firm.

PAST PERFORMANCE AS AN EVALUATION FACTOR IN SOURCE SELECTION

Government contract awards are based on the evaluation factors and subfactors stated in solicitations. These criteria should represent key areas relevant to the work being purchased under the awarded contract. Ideally, these source selection factors support meaningful offeror comparisons and provide the ability to discriminate between offerors. The government is required to state the factors clearly in the solicitation, and potential bidders must respond meticulously to the factors stated in the solicitation.

The specific criteria on which a company will be assessed are described in the issued solicitation. All solicitations must describe the evaluation approach, provide opportunities to identify past or current contracts, and allow offerors to provide information on problems encountered and the corrective actions that were taken.

Thorough company past performance evaluation, including information outside submitted proposals, ensures that awards are made to good performers over good proposal writers. Proposal narratives must be supported by proven results. High-quality evaluation criteria are few in number and are linked to critical performance standards and specifically the seller's ability to handle all critical risks reflected in the statement of work. Those criteria will be used to meaningfully discriminate between bidders. Each factor should be a variable with measurable variance that the agency will use to compare various companies' results in past projects against the stated evaluation criteria.

Evaluation factors should be as independent of one other as possible to avoid redundancy or repetition that will weaken comparisons and result in a factor's being considered a weakness in multiple areas—an issue that is often discussed at the factor level but can arise at the subfactor level. It is relatively easy for an RFP author or acquisition strategy creator to unintentionally blur distinctions between technical evaluation scores and past performance assessments at the subfactor level and end up with multiple evaluation criteria assessing the same attribute (for example, including a management and staffing response from offerors that is evaluated and requiring that proposed staff are included in the past performance response). The result is that strengths and weaknesses can be counted twice or overemphasized in the evaluation. This practice is to be avoided, because it has resulted in sustained protests.

Basic Requirements

Generally speaking, past performance evaluations are conducted by the same government team that evaluates the technical proposal. The evaluator may be either a single individual or an assigned team, such as a technical evaluation board or source selection evaluation board. Regardless of whether an individual or team evaluates past performance, it will be comparatively evaluated against a predetermined scale or, infrequently, on a pass/fail basis.

Past performance and other source selection evaluations are frequently conducted as "award on initial proposals," where there is no opportunity for dialogue between offerors and the evaluating agency during the time between proposal submission and award decision. Astute offerors always plan on this being the case and do not assume there will be an opportunity for discussions or clarifications regarding their submitted proposals. However, the government is required to provide an opportunity for bidders to comment on adverse past performance information uncovered during source selection.

Government buyers seek to measure and evaluate confidence in an offeror's ability to perform successfully based on previous and current contract efforts. Government past performance evaluators typically consider the currency and relevance of the information being reviewed, the source and context of information, and general trends in contractor performance. Also included in source selection past performance evaluation are the use of past performance information regarding predecessor companies, key personnel, and proposed subcontractors.

Past Performance Evaluation Rules

Two rules must be adhered to during the evaluation process. These rules address (1) disclosure of adverse past performance information and (2) revealing sources of past performance information.

Offerors must be provided the opportunity to address any adverse past performance information. Some offerors are aware of adverse information ahead of time and address it in their initial proposals. Some may not be aware of any adverse information when their references send inputs directly to the government agency conducting the evaluation, not to the offeror.

The government agency cannot reveal the names of individuals providing reference information about an offeror's past performance. This ensures that the process remains honest and non-confrontational. A good way to avoid concerns with adverse evaluations is to set up a meeting with past clients to make sure that they are absolutely satisfied with every aspect of the working relationship they had with the firm, before using them as a reference for a past performance evaluation.

Section M Evaluation Criteria

Federal government RFPs follow a standard format consisting of 13 sections labeled *A* through *M*. Section *M* states the evaluation criteria and evaluation method to be used to make a contract award decision. Evaluation of the performance risk associated with contract award to a firm is at the core of a past performance evaluation. In general terms, a past performance evaluation has four aspects:

1. Management performance of the specified relevant contracts
2. Quality of the products or services delivered
3. Adherence to schedule requirements
4. Cost control performance on the specified relevant contracts.

Management performance of the specified relevant contracts involves a thorough and thoughtful evaluation of the firm that managed the project, how it performed that function, and if it has the ability to manage the project it is bidding on in the same capacity.

Quality of the products or services delivered addresses exactly what it implies. If the quality of products and services in the past has been less than exceptional, the offeror should clearly show why that has changed, list the exact steps undertaken to ensure the changes have been upheld, and give confidence that low quality will not happen again. This is a very challenging obstacle to overcome and one where proof of quality correction should be provided.

Adherence to schedule requirements plays a significant part in past performance evaluations. Government agencies are very specific and particular about projects being on time. It can be rather tricky at times, because a contractor may not have control over some delays in the schedule, yet is accountable for adhering to all schedule requirements. Clear documentation that shows factual reasons why delays happened is the best way to counteract the possible negative impact of non-adherence to schedule requirements.

Cost control performance on specified relevant contracts shows that a company can stay within the budgeted parameters of the project, or better yet show a consistent history of coming in below budget. Government agencies seeking a contractor want to be assured they are receiving the best possible product or service at an even better price.

Relevance of Past Performance Information

The *source selection authority*, which is often the contracting officer, is the party that determines the relevance of past performance information. It will normally consider such things as the nature of the business areas involved, required levels of technology, contract types, similarity of materials and products, location of work to be performed, and similarity in size, scope, and complexity of the project.

All of these considerations, in part or whole, will help the source selection authority determine whether the proposal being reviewed presents past performance projects that meet the solicitation criteria for the project being bid on. This reinforces the urgency of preparing accurate, detailed, and factually correct information for the submitted proposal. Like most things prepared by people, there is significant variation in how well past projects are detailed and described.

Section M Past Performance Evaluation Scheme Example

While there is considerable latitude in how preparers craft and arrange the different parts of a solicitation, the evaluation schemes presented in Section M typically conform to a standard format. A Section M past performance evaluation scheme used by a government agency in 2012 is provided in Exhibit 5-A.

CLIENT PERCEPTIONS

A potential client's perception of a company is extremely important. Companies are well served by using their proposals to align their experience, branding, and messaging with one another. A business known primarily for building barrels may have a difficult time being perceived as a serious candidate for a project that involves building circuit boards. A business with messaging devoted to innovation through disruption of existing processes and technologies may face an uphill battle with a prospective client evaluation of a proposal to an agency most concerned with minimizing risk and maximizing continuity of program support.

In the age of instant information, firms must make sure they show their strengths through all communication channels: websites, social media, industry-specific trade journals, job boards, and other forums where there is activity linkable to the company. Failure to do this can result in poor client perceptions and past performance ratings because the necessary experience will be difficult, if not impossible, to verify. It would be a rare and unique situation where a company that builds barrels could also participate in a project that builds circuit boards, but this level of diversification of service offerings is not unheard of. Prospective clients will seek to verify claims about who a firm is and what it has done.

In the following sections, we discuss the buyer viewpoints most commonly encountered in a government client: the contracting officer, the contract specialist, the requirement owner, and the contracting officer's representative. It is important to note that any one "viewpoint" or singular point of interaction with a prospective client does not tell the whole story. The viewpoint of a prospective client is an aggregate of the viewpoints of multiple parties who may or may not be in agreement about what is needed, who will have differing levels of influence, and who vary in their assignment of importance to any particular issue, among other differences.

Contracting Officer

A contracting officer is the individual who has the authority to bind the United States government to a contract in an amount greater than the micropurchase threshold ($3,000, with exceptions, as of June 2014). If this person does not have a favorable perception of the company that is bidding on the project, he or she is not likely to sign off on the contract. Contracting officers have the final say in contract award decisions and are ultimately responsible for awarding a contract to the best qualified bidder on the project. The contracting officer is also ultimately responsible for awarded contracts being fulfilled according to the agreed-upon terms.

The contracting officer is also the party that is most likely to have written or created the acquisition strategy, the solicitation, and specifically the instructions to offerors and evaluation criteria, including the sections on past performance. In larger buying organizations, some of these activities and documents will have been created by teams or by a group that includes more specialized divisions of responsibility. In smaller organizations and for procurements that are smaller in dollar value, the contracting officer is more likely to have personally authored all of these documents (if they are used). Larger agencies (in particular DoD) also may have further divisions of labor and designations among contracting officers, with some dedicated to the initial procurement (procuring contracting officer), to the administration of contracts (administrative contracting officer), or to terminating contracts (terminating contracting officer).

Contract Specialist

In terms of procurement authority, a contract specialist is a designee of the contracting officer. The specialist may or may not have a warrant to sign as a contracting officer on a limited (hence the term "limited warrant") basis. In many cases, a contracting officer will lead a team of contract specialists who manage acquisitions under the authority of the contracting officer, who is the signatory on procurement artifacts such as prenegotiation memoranda, solicitations, and contracts. A contract specialist may be indistinguishable from a contracting officer, from a seller's perspective. He or she may also be distinguishable as a gatekeeper, without the authority to say "yes" or having such authority only under a specific and limited set of circumstances. A contract specialist can in some cases act as a filter between the seller and the person or persons in the buying organization with the authority and responsibility to conduct an acquisition or specific procurement.

Requirement Owner

Requirement owner as used here refers to the party or parties responsible for government program execution, at least enough to be responsible for accomplishment of a particular scope of work. Some or all of this work may be acquired from or contracted for from sellers, meaning from someone other than the agency itself (which may include other government agencies or private sellers). Requirement owners are typically in line or mission organizations and frequently have program or project manager backgrounds and experience bases. They may come from a variety of disciplines which are, ideally, aligned with the requirement or scope of work in question. Requirement owners articulate their requirements in statements of work, statements of objectives, performance work statements (PWSs) and other documents and artifacts that define the purpose behind the requirement, the requirement itself, and desired outcomes. Requirement owners rely on contracting officers and specialists to perform the brokering needed to achieve completion of their requirements—not an abdication of responsibility, but rather a shared responsibility.

Contracting Officer's Representative

The *contracting officer's representative* (COR) is a role usually filled by the requiring agency or activity (which is frequently distinct and separate from the contracting activity). The COR is delegated specific authority by the contracting officer and is typically responsible for certain administrative activities and for monitoring performance under an awarded contract. CORs are rarely if ever given authority to modify or make changes to a contract. They are typically performance monitors who accept deliverables, approve invoices, and provide technical direction within the scope of the awarded contract.

In many cases, the COR is indistinguishable from the requirements owner. In other cases, the COR role is limited to very specific duties. Of course, there are many variations across this spectrum of COR responsibility, and historically, assignment as a COR has been a collateral duty. Recently, agencies have been hiring and assigning CORs as full-time employees. The Office of Federal Procurement Policy Act (41 U.S.C. § 401) assigns responsibility and authority to the Federal Acquisition Institute (FAI) to promote and develop a professional federal acquisition workforce. Acting under this commission, the FAI has implemented certification and career development programs, including a three-tiered certification program for civilian agencies, and specifically has a certification scheme for CORs.

COLLECTION METHODS

Past performance questionnaires are very frequently required in solicitations by government buying agencies that include a direct response from client references to the government. The primary collection method used is to provide offerors with a past performance questionnaire or survey form without any other solicitation documents; the offeror selects clients to ask to fill out and return directly to the contracting officer, typically via email. Web-enabled surveys are rarely used.

These questionnaires rarely, if ever, benefit from the robust body of knowledge and best practices that exist for the design, layout, and response formats of surveys and questionnaires. The result is that the majority of government past performance questionnaires used in government solicitations create unnecessary work for bidders, for questionnaire respondents, for those collecting and collating responses, and for those evaluating responses. More troubling than the unnecessary work, though, is that most government past performance questionnaires used in government solicitations are developed with a lack of regard for survey basics such as respondent bias, leading questions, and balance in response scales.

The primary source of performance information government agencies use for evaluation outside submitted proposals is contained in repositories such as CPARS and PPIRS. Another method less often used than past performance questionnaires in government solicitations is to have the offerors provide client references and contact information. The government agency then calls or emails the referents to either ask them directly about the performance of the offeror or ask them to complete some form of a questionnaire. A standard in government solicitations is to restate that in addition to past performance information provided by the offeror, the government may consider information from other sources in its evaluation of past performance. As an (unidentified) 2012 DoD solicitation Section M states,

> the evaluation of past performance will be performed using all relevant information that is readily available to the Government including both the information received from Offerors and the information obtained from other sources. During the evaluation of an Offeror's past performance, the Government may query the Government agency references provided by the Offeror. Other sources may include interviews with program managers and contracting officers, available DoD and other agency past performance databases and available data from previous source selections or contractor capability assessments.

One of the richest and arguably the best sources of past performance Information is first-hand ("close-at-hand") knowledge by a client agency of a contractor's performance with them. GAO has confirmed that the use of close-at-hand knowledge about an offeror regarding its past performance is a requirement: If an evaluating activity is or should have been aware of the past performance of an offeror, then it must take that information into consideration in its past performance evaluation.[15]

The pros and cons of various collection methods and formats are summarized in Table 5-1.

Method or Format of Collection	Pros	Cons
PP filled out by seller	Sellers have opportunity to explain relevancy and other elements of PP Levels playing field by keeping response control in hands of sellers	Seller bias in client selection Seller complete control of PP narrative

---

[15] GTS Duratek, Inc., GAO B-280511.2, 1998; www.gao.gov/products/402719#mt= e-report.

Method or Format of Collection	Pros	Cons
PPQ filled out by seller-selected client(s)	Seller provides hard-to-find information; contacts and identifying information of relevant PP PPI provided by referent with lessened seller influence	Seller bias in client selection Reluctance of referents to complete and timely submit PPQ Uneven playing field by factor not under control of seller (PPQ completion)
Retrieve from CPARS/PPIRS or other buyer repository	Eliminates seller bias in selection and responses Relative ease of access and collection of PPI Takes advantage of previously collected PPI	Incomplete PPI or no PPI in system on contracts and contractor performance Information in repository likely to be vague or neutral ratings
Seller provides PP contact information, buyer calls or emails references	Eliminates seller bias in responses Seller provides hard-to-find information; contacts and identifying information of relevant PP	Seller bias in client selection Burden of PPI collection on buyer
Interviews	Eliminates seller bias in responses Increased fidelity of responses	Labor-intensive PPI collection Burden of PPI collection on buyer Increased chance of uneven data collection across referents and offerors
Award/incentive fee plans	Takes advantage of previously collected PPI	Infrequently used contract type limits use as source History of inflated ratings in incentive and award fee ratings Contracts, points of contact, ratings and narratives not in central repository and not easily found

Method or Format of Collection	Pros	Cons
Agency collection during performance on specific contract	Minimizes seller bias in selection and responses Collection and ratings assigned occur closer to actual performance	Information in repository likely to be vague or neutral ratings
Handwritten forms	Easier for respondents most comfortable with hard copy forms and handwritten responses Higher comfort factor for buyer evaluators most comfortable with hard copy forms and handwritten responses	Most difficult to process except in cases of very few offerors and PPQs Burden on respondents to convert formats (print, write, scan, mail, email, etc.) for submission Potentially difficult to read/interpret responses
Electronic submission of emailed form	Takes advantage of most-used communications channel Depending on format used, may facilitate compilation of responses and evaluation with narratives and ratings that are copy-capable	Burden on respondents to (download, complete, email, etc.) for submission Reluctance of referents to complete and timely submit PPQ
Electronic response via survey or other web-enabled response format	Enhanced user interfaces that allow completion at user pace and choice of location Advanced analytics of responses and automated follow-up and other administrative tools to manage collection	Government recipients of web survey may have access issues related to their degree of access to the Internet from work locations Collecting activity has to learn/understand tool being used

Table 5-1: Pros and Cons of Past Performance Information (PPI) Sources, Collection Methods, and Formats

*Table responses are predicated on the use of standardized response format for all collection methods, including use of an interview guide for interviews.

ASSESSING PAST PERFORMANCE WRITE-UPS

When should a company first create a past performance write-up? The moment the contract is awarded! A past performance write-up can begin with the insertion of the statement of work from the awarded contract. If you reflect on this point for a moment, you may realize that the moment the proposal is written is a great time to record the first pass at a past performance write-up. Chances are that at this moment, the statement of work has been studied more than it will ever be and the company has devoted the creative energy of its best and brightest talent to planning how the company will knock it out of the park during contract performance. This is an excellent time to put these elements into a past performance write-up that can then be refined and improved.

There are a number of ways to self-assess a past performance write-up. These range from how relevant the past performance is to how well it is written. The past performance ranking tool in Figure 5-1 was devised to aid in making a serious, thoughtful, and thorough review of a past performance write-up.

Using the past performance ranking tool can help with three things:

1. Guiding an in-depth assessment of a past performance write-up

2. Providing insight on specific ways to improve a past performance write-up

3. Assessing company fit for a particular project or team.

Past Performance Ranking:
- Rank PP with mark on each line
- More marks further right is better
- Use to decide between which PP to use in bid, or to guide rewrite of PP citation

Opportunity	Past Performance	Evaluator	Date

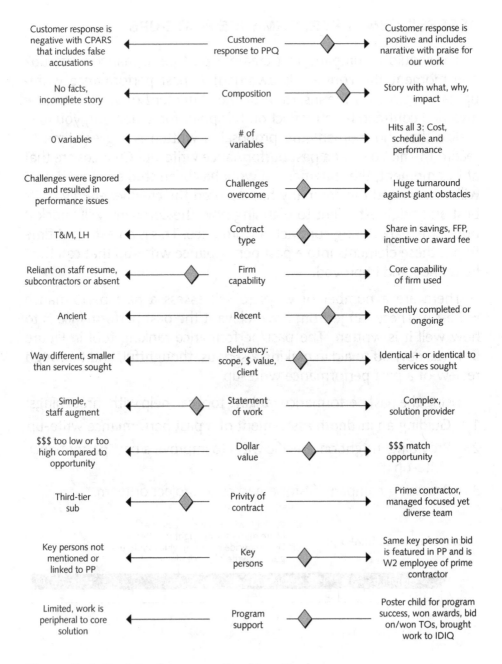

Figure 5-1: Past Performance Ranking Tool

Diamond symbols illustrate ratings of past performance on each spectra, showing that ratings may differ.

A self-assessment of a past performance write-up that leads to the determination that the particular write-up, or the past performance underlying the write-up, is not a good fit for this particular proposal is not a black or white judgment on the use of the information. When a company has a great experience it wishes to share, but the experience does not reflect the parameters of the proposed project or is missing important relevancy or other attributes, it can still serve as a proof statement in a proposal or in other materials. A proof statement is just what it sounds like: a statement that backs up a claim by providing proof to the claim, that what is being proposed or marketed has been done before to some degree of success.

The ranking system for past performance involves marks given on a Likert scale for each category. The farther right the marks, the more favorably it is viewed. Likewise, the farther left the marks, the more likely it is to be viewed negatively in that category.

This evaluation tool is designed to provide understanding and awareness of the significance of all aspects of a past performance write-up, plus a clearer perspective of what the government is looking for when evaluating a company for a project. The highest utility achieved with this tool comes when it has been tailored to the specific requirements in a solicitation and is used to evaluate and improve past performance write-ups before inclusion in a proposal.

The use of the tool is relatively straightforward. Tailor the spectra for the circumstances at hand (a specific solicitation perhaps) and rank the write-up with a mark on each line. Use this tool to decide which past performance to use in a bid, to guide rewriting of a past performance citation, or to assess and select team members against a specific set of criteria associated with a business opportunity. The more marks further to the right, the better.

There are 13 spectra with subjective scales for each from left to right.

Customer Response to Past Performance Questionnaire

The government collects information via past performance questionnaires (PPQ)s provided to bidders; the bidders give the forms to their clients to complete. However, clients do not send their answers back to the company, but directly to the government for review. This can be scary ground if a business is unsure of the outcome of that PPQ. It does not have the opportunity to submit ten, then pick and choose the best three out of ten responses. Obviously, firms would be remiss if they did not talk to past clients long before a PPQ is sent to ensure they would be able to give the highest possible ratings on a PPQ. If any client says it could not do this, that is the ideal time for the company to find out why and what steps they can take immediately to improve their performance and make potential scores higher.

Composition

A past performance write-up is a story about a firm's past performance that it provides to a party who is interested in hiring for a new project. Like all great stories, it needs to have a hero or protagonist with an obstacle or challenge to overcome. And the story also has to have an ending. Positive endings are a must—there are no notable examples of negative endings that delivered somebody a new government contract! Think of how a positive story captures attention and draws the reader in. People and government agencies alike tend to distance themselves from negative endings.

By the end of the write-up, the story should express the impact created by that company for its client. It needs to clearly establish that it knows how to manage business contracts and deliver beyond the minimum expectations.

Number of Variables

Number of variables refers to any conditions that impact the contract and how a company can manage them. Cost, schedule, and performance are the three main contract variables—these are certain to be considered when any proposal is being scrutinized and reviewed. Regardless of perspective (e.g., agency or contractor), the questions asked in analyzing a past performance can include:

- How much money was spent to achieve a certain objective?
- Was the project on schedule?
- Did performance improve?
- Have the results of the project created more efficiency or effectiveness?
- Does the past performance show how a company saved money for the client, finished ahead of schedule, and performed well or provided an above-average outcome?

If the variables do not sing a company's praises and celebrate its positive accomplishment, that is a bad sign. The variables need to reflect a positive impact; any variables that do not support a positive impact should be avoided or downplayed in the write-up if at all possible.

Challenges Overcome

It bears repeating that the government likes to hear a sound and factually correct story about how a firm overcame a challenge to achieve success. The past performance write-up must include great stories that show how this has happened. Talk about how the challenge arose, describe the response, and show how this response conquered that problem.

If a firm is examining its past performance and does not believe it has had challenges, this can mean a couple of things. It could be in denial, or it simply took jobs that did not challenge it, so surpassing goals was not difficult. These are extremely unlikely occurrences, however, and savvy evaluators will not consider them favorably.

Another element firms can address when they are expressing how they overcame challenges is their weaknesses. Give examples of each of them. An effective writer or verbal communicator can adequately portray a weakness and the impact of that weakness. For example, a perfectionist may note how that perfectionism carries over into their work at times and makes them over-analytical; however, that may not be unappealing to someone who knows his project will receive a high level of attention from you. You can portray a weakness honestly and show that you are aware of it but that it does not hinder what you can do.

When writing about past challenges, firms should highlight projects that show they were hired when a program was in arrears, out of cost control, behind schedule, missing big deliverables, or some other negative. Build your story around how you turned the program around, got it functioning efficiently and effectively, perhaps even won an award, and overall made a positive contribution that left that program undeniably in better condition. That will give you a rating on the right side of the scale. Firms can expect to be on the left side of the scale if they cannot provide such verifiable, detailed stories of success.

Contract Type

There are three basic types of contracts to understand when pursuing a contract with a government agency: cost plus, firm-fixed price (FFP), and time and materials (T&M). The assessment line in the past performance ranking tool shows examples of contract types on the two extremes. The further to the right, the more complicated the contract or the greater the weight of the performance risk on the contractor.

On a fundamental level, contracts allocate risk between buyer and seller. FFP contracts place all risk on the contractor, whereas T&M contracts place all the risk on the government. When firms evaluate their past performance, they need to assess which ones tell a better story in the context of contract type; one more closely matching the contemplated new contract arrangement, or portraying the contractor past performance in successfully managing a more complex contract, or showing the contractor taking on higher risk than the government. Elements such as advanced program and project management, incentive and award fee structures, or other rewards or penalties tied to performance, will tell a strong story of a company's confidence in the results it delivers.

Other, less common contract features that may help improve the rating in this area are the reinvestment of cost savings in technologies or future development and the contractor's accepting a small percentage of the achieved savings as compensation, as in share-in-savings and some incentive fee arrangements.

Firm Capability

The primary measuring stick in this area is how closely the past performance write-up aligns with the core capability of the firm. Unless complex program management of subcontractors is one of the skills required by a solicitation, a past performance write-up that indicates that the brunt of the effort was borne by subcontractors or temporary staff is less credible than one showing that the work a firm performed is directly aligned with its core capabilities.

Buyers want to hire the best and most qualified contractors. The government views firm capability in the same light. A firm's core capability must be presented and easily identified and confirmed. If a firm says in its proposal that it is the best boat builder in the area, do sources of information available to the buyer corroborate that? If the business is called Jim's Boat Yard and it has submitted a proposal with the government or is expecting to attract boatyard customers, its marketplace presence and all associated manifestations (e.g., client references, online presence) should confirm that it has boatyard capabilities. If not, the firm has a branding and identity problem that may cause less-than-ideal perceptions and lowered evaluations of either the relevancy or merit of its past performance.

Imagine that the evaluating individual or team at the government agency is reviewing Jim's Boat Yard's proposal. The team is impressed and believes that the firm is the real deal. Jim's a naval architect, has a team that's been with him for years, and has been the premier boat builder in the area for nearly 30 years.

The proposal review team picks up the next proposal and it's from Big Bob's Wrecking Yard. That doesn't sound like it has anything to do with ship building. The team digs further for details. The website doesn't say a thing about building ships; however, it has some awesome pictures of gigantic wrecking balls destroying buildings. What's the connection? The reviewer looks further and finds that Big Bob believes that wrecking things isn't so far off from building boats: You have to be meticulous, careful, organized, and knowledgeable in using and disposing of dangerous materials. And Bob's cousin Vinnie just finished whittling a canoe in woodshop class!

Would you trust the core capabilities of Jim's Boat Yard or Big Bob's Wrecking Yard? That is not a difficult decision—unless complex program management of subcontractors is one of the skills required. The government needs to know what a firm can control without relying on second- or third-tier contractors. It's not that subcontractors won't be used, but that Big Bob doesn't have any expertise in overseeing a boatbuilding project.

Recency

Companies must have past performance evaluations that are recent: A firm's "moment of glory" contract from 20 years ago doesn't cut the mustard anymore. The solicitation should provide specific parameters regarding *how recent* cited projects need to be. Projects that are ongoing or recently completed will rank to the right more than ones that were completed long ago.

One way for firms to improve their recency score is to offer warranties or no-cost follow-ups. (It's a great sales tool as well.) Firms should make a phone call to stay in touch or stop by to check things out. That gesture allows firms to have recent or ongoing contact with past clients, and that prolonging of the engagement may move their scores to the right or otherwise enable them to cite a past performance that otherwise would be too old to use.

Relevancy

Relevancy has three key aspects: scope, dollar value, and client. Ideally, firms will have performance with the same or similar scope, dollar value, and client. This comes down to compatibility: A bidding firm needs to show that it can relate to and work on the scale of the project out for bids by submitting "relevant" (i.e., similar in scope, value, and client) past performance stories and evaluations. If a firm is small and has only done a $20,000 job but is bidding on a $1 million project with no proven experience of handling a project of that size, that will potentially reflect negatively on it and move the firm to the left of the scale.

If a company has one aspect of relevancy that is weaker than the others, there still may be ways to emphasize similarity. For example, a firm may be bidding on a U.S. Secret Service project. Its past performance evaluations include projects for the Federal Air Marshal Service and the U.S. Marine Corps. Which of those is more similar? At first glance, the firm's experience may seem generally incompatible. But a likely answer is that the Air Marshals contract performance makes a better fit. Although the Secret Service protects a specific person and the Air Marshals protect all air travelers, they have similar missions—to ensure public safety. Furthermore, both use firearms in a civilian context and are given certain authority to act according to their missions, while very seldom does the Marine Corps work in a civilian context or in principal protection.

Statement of Work

A statement of work details the timeline, deliverables, and tasks or work activities a contractor has completed or that it will execute under a contract. Statements of work from past performances need to fit the statement of work being bid on. The assessment scale in Figure 5-1 puts tasks that involve providing complex solutions on the right. The far left would show simple solutions or staff augmentation. Complex solutions show that the contractor was responsible for development and design of a solution that was successful; this doesn't have to be a tangible object, because it could also be a process. Simple solutions and staff augmentations include situations where the government was responsible for finding the solution and the contractor helped implement it with no responsibility for ensuring its success. The statement of work and the solicitation being bid on will most likely show these distinctions. A consideration in examining complexity is to match the complexity of the prospective past performance citation to that of the effort being proposed on.

Dollar Value

The dollar values a company presents for past projects are best if they match the project being bid on. In general, dollar value is best when it is 100%–120% of the bid amount, rather than below (or much higher than) the bid amount. If the solicitation allows a company to present three past performances, projects should be chosen to show an ideal dollar value mix: one project that was 100 percent of the bid value, another 120 percent, and the third 110 percent. If a company must have one that is below the bid amount, it should keep it as close as possible.

Privity of Contract

Privity of contract refers to the legal relationship and responsibilities between the two parties to a contract: Only the buyer and seller (i.e., government and contractor) have rights and obligations under the contract. Prime contractors have privity of contract with subcontractors, while no legal relationship exists between a subcontractor and the government, because there is no direct contract between them.

It is better to show direct privity (i.e., direct experience) with the government or other cited client than with another firm as a subcontractor. Past performance citations where the bidder was the prime contractor and has shown that it actively managed its team and subcontractors are generally perceived and rated more positively. Direct experience with the government shows higher-level management experience and responsibility.

At the opposite end, if a firm has typically been a lower-tier subcontractor, it may be too disconnected from a project. It may have performed or provided staff augmentation roles as opposed to solution provider roles. It is important in a past performance write-up where a firm performed as a subcontractor to closely document involvement in contract performance and show that it was an essential, integral part of the project's success.

Key Persons

Government solicitations and contracts may specify *key personnel*, wherein key positions are identified; this requires the following: (1) resumes of proposed key persons, (2) letters of commitment or contingent letters of offer and acceptance, (3) demonstration that proposed key personnel are qualified to perform the work, and (4) that key persons must remain on the job some minimum amount of time after award, such as 90 days, barring a catastrophic event (e.g., accidents or death). These provisions are put in solicitations and contracts by buyers to ensure that the winning contractor will not use personnel less qualified than those described and evaluated in the winning proposal during contract performance.

This can be a tricky point for proposals. Typically, key persons are not requested to be mentioned nor are they typically mentioned in past performance write-ups; however, that doesn't mean that a firm can't or shouldn't include them. If key persons are proposed in a bid, and these same key persons were a part of the past performance being cited, this past performance will score higher. Ideally, these key people would be W2 employees or prominent in the firm (e.g., the founder of the company).

If a proposal does cite key people, make sure it gives specific examples of what they will bring to the project to demonstrate their value. A word of caution: *Make sure the key people cited will be a part of the current project.* Proposing specific people and subsequently failing to deliver them sets the stage for a poor client reference from the project. Key persons who are current employees of the prime contractor bidding the work typically rate higher than alternatives, such as new hires contingent upon contract award or temporary staff.

On the opposite end, firms that do not have any key people to showcase in the past performance write-up may rank lower as a result. But firms may be a bit to the left in the ranking and still not be negatively impacted if they propose using a subcontractor they have previously used successfully on multiple projects. Remember, making promises in a proposal that cannot be kept is problematic for a firm's reputation.

Program Support

The level of program support a firm provided on a project is important. Ranking on the right side of the spectrum in Figure 5-1 will indicate a model of success, probably supported by awards and acclamations. When a company did much of the work that resulted in these accolades, it speaks well about its abilities as a contractor.

On the left side of the program support spectrum will be the firm whose involvement was limited and whose work didn't contribute to gaining recognition for the client or project. This is where the subcontractor that was behind the scenes or doing off-site work will end up—definitely "out of sight, out of mind."

Example Solicitation Critique

Exhibit 5-B provides an example of a past performance evaluation scheme that includes the instructions provided to offerors by an agency in a draft RFP. This extreme example was an actual 2013 solicitation, and it is provided along with a critique by a prospective bidder to offer an additional real-world example of the potential impacts of choices made regarding past performance collection methods and formats.

Exhibit 5-A: Section M Past Performance Evaluation Scheme

FACTOR 2: Past Performance

State Relative Importance: Less important than the Technical/Management Approach Factor.

The past performance evaluation factor assesses the degree of confidence the government has in an offeror's ability to supply products and services that meet users' needs, including cost and schedule, based on a demonstrated record of performance for efforts similar to the government requirement.

Performance confidence is assessed at the overall past performance factor level, whereas recency, relevancy, and quality of the offeror's past performance are assessed for each individual past performance effort.

Recency Assessment: Recent contracts are defined as those contracts presently being performed or which have been performed during the past three (3) years from the date of issuance of this solicitation. Past performance information that fails this condition will not be evaluated.

Relevancy Assessment: If the government evaluators consider the offeror's past performance reference to be recent, then the government will assess the relevancy of the referenced past performance task order/contract. The government determines relevancy by evaluating the past performance references against the technical factor/subfactors contained in the solicitation. The past performance factor does not contain subfactors. The past performance information obtained from other sources will be used to establish the degree of relevancy and quality of past performance.

For each instance of an offeror's past performance that meets the recency timeframe, the evaluators will then assess relevancy of that instance of past performance. In this part of the evaluation, the evaluators assess a relevancy rating utilizing the past performance Relevancy Definitions (see table) focusing on and targeting performance which is relevant to Technical/Management subfactors. Evaluators do not assess an overall relevancy rating at the factor level. Further, the government is not bound by the offeror's opinion of relevancy.

Past Performance Relevancy Definitions**

Relevancy	Definition
Very Relevant	Present/past performance effort involved similar scope and magnitude of effort and complexities this solicitation requires.
Somewhat Relevant	Present/past performance effort involved some of the scope and magnitude of effort and complexities this solicitation requires.
Not Relevant	Present/past performance effort involved little or none of the scope and magnitude of effort and complexities this solicitation requires.

** The past performance evaluation will be accomplished by reviewing aspects of an offeror's recent and relevant present/past performance. For each instance of past performance, the evaluators will first determine if the individual effort meets the recency definition set forth in the RFQ/RFP. Past performance information that fails this condition will not be evaluated. However, if any part of the performance falls within the recency time frame, the contract/task order in its entirety may be evaluated.

Quality Assessment Rating*

Rating	Description
EXCEPTIONAL (E)	During the contract period, contractor performance meets or met contractual requirements and exceeds or exceeded many to the Government's benefit. The contractual performance of the element or sub-element being assessed was accomplished with few minor problems for which corrective actions taken by the contractor were highly effective.
VERY GOOD (VG)	During the contract period, contractor performance meets or met contractual requirements and exceeds or exceeded some to the Government's benefit. The contractual performance of the element or sub-element being assessed was accomplished with some minor problems for which corrective actions taken by the contractor were effective.
SATISFACTORY (S)	During the contract period, contractor performance meets or met contractual requirements. The contractual performance of the element or sub-element being assessed contained some minor problems for which corrective actions taken by the contractor appear or were satisfactory.
MARGINAL (M)	During the contract period, contractor performance does not or did not meet some contractual requirements. The contractual performance of the element or sub-element being assessed reflects a serious problem for which the contractor has not yet identified corrective actions. The contractor's proposed actions appear only marginally effective or were not fully implemented.
UNSATISFACTORY(U)	During the contract period, contractor performance does not or did not meet most contractual requirements and recovery in a timely manner is not likely. The contractual performance of the element or sub-element contains serious problem(s) for which the contractor's corrective actions appear or were ineffective.
NOT APPLICABLE (N)	Unable to provide a rating. Contract did not include performance for this aspect. Do not know.

*** Performance Quality Assessment. After recency and relevancy have been determined, the government will assess the quality of each of the referenced past performance efforts. The quality assessment may consist of an evaluation of the past performance questionnaire responses, interviews with government customers and fee determining officials, and if applicable, commercial clients. Past performance information may be obtained from any other sources available to the government, to include, but not limited to, the Past Performance Information Retrieval System (PPIRS), Federal Awardee Performance and Integrity Information System (FAPIIS), Electronic Subcontract Reporting System (eSRS), or other databases; interviews with program managers, contracting officers, and fee determining officials; and the Defense Contract Management Agency. The past performance evaluation team will review this past performance information and determine the quality and usefulness as it applies to performance confidence assessment.

Performance Confidence Assessment**

Rating	Description
Substantial Confidence	Based on the offeror's recent/relevant performance record, the government has a high expectation that the offeror will successfully perform the required effort.
Satisfactory Confidence	Based on the offeror's recent/relevant performance record, the government has a reasonable expectation that the offeror will successfully perform the required effort.
Limited Confidence	Based on the offeror's recent/relevant performance record, the government has a low expectation that the offeror will successfully perform the required effort.
No Confidence	Based on the offeror's recent/relevant performance record, the government has no expectation that the offeror will be able to successfully perform the required effort.
Unknown Confidence (Neutral)	No recent/relevant performance record is available or the offeror's performance record is so sparse that no meaningful confidence assessment rating can be reasonably assigned.

**** As a result of the recency, relevancy, and quality assessments, the government evaluation team will then assign an integrated performance confidence assessment rating from the Performance Confidence Assessment table (Table 5-3). The resulting performance confidence assessment rating is made at the past performance factor level and represents an overall evaluation of contractor performance.

More relevant performance will have a greater impact on the Performance Confidence Assessment than a less relevant effort. A strong record of relevant past performance may be considered more advantageous to the government than an "Unknown Confidence" rating. Likewise, a more relevant past performance record may receive a higher confidence rating and be considered more favorably than a less relevant record of favorable performance.

Exhibit 5-B: Example Solicitation Critique

The following is an excerpt of a solicitation issued in 2013 by a federal agency.

RFP Section A Page 2:

9. Paragraph L-25, Volume II past performance File Content, paragraph (4) requires offerors to e-mail the past performance Assessment Questionnaire at Attachment 0003 of this solicitation to all contractual, technical, and administrative points of contact for each contract submitted in the past performance proposal. Offerors must ensure that this is accomplished in sufficient time for assessments to be completed and submitted to the contracting officer prior to the date and time set for receipt of proposals.

RFP Section L Pages 71-72:

Volume II past performance File Content.

Offerors shall submit a list of relevant Federal Government contracts (prime contracts, task/delivery orders, and/or major subcontracts in performance during the past two years from the date of issuance of the final solicitation), which are relevant to the services and supplies required by this solicitation. Data concerning the prime Offeror shall be provided first, followed by each of the top three proposed major subcontractors (e.g.,the top three anticipated performers from a cost perspective), in alphabetical order. This volume shall be organized into the following sections:

(1)   Section 1 Contract Descriptions

    (a)   Contractor/Subcontractor place of performance, CAGE Code and DUNS Number. If the work was performed as a subcontractor, also provide the name of the prime contractor and Point of Contact (POC) within the prime contractor organization (name, and current address, e-mail address, and telephone and fax numbers).

    (b)   Federal Government contracting activity, and current address, Procuring contracting officer's name, e-mail address, telephone and fax numbers.

    (c)   Governments technical representative/COR, and current e-mail address, telephone and fax numbers.

    (d)   Government contract administration activity and the Administrative contracting officer's name, and current e-mail address, telephone and fax numbers.

    (e)   Contract Number and, in the case of Indefinite Delivery type contracts, GSA contracts, and Blanket Purchase Agreements, include Delivery Order Numbers also.

    (f)   Contract Type (specific type such as Firm Fixed Price (FFP) or Cost Plus Fixed Fee (CPFF)). In the case of Indefinite Delivery contracts, indicate specific type (Requirements, Definite Quantity, and Indefinite Quantity) and secondary contract type (FFP, CPFF).

    (g)   Awarded price/cost.

    (h)   Final or projected final price/cost.

(i)   Original delivery schedule, including dates of start and completion of work.

(j)   Final or projected final delivery schedule, including dates of start and completion of work.

(2)   Section 2 - Performance

Offerors shall provide a specific narrative explanation of each contract listed in Section 1, describing the objectives achieved and detailing how the effort is relevant to the requirements of this solicitation. For any contract(s)/task order(s) that did not/do not meet original schedule or technical performance requirements, provide a brief explanation of the reason(s) for the shortcoming(s) and any corrective action(s) taken to avoid recurrence. The Offerors shall list each time the delivery schedule was revised and provide an explanation of why the revision was necessary. All Requests for Deviation and Requests for Waiver shall be addressed with respect to causes and corrective actions. The Offerors shall also provide a copy of any Cure Notices or Show Cause Letters received on each contract listed and a description of any corrective action implemented by the Offeror. The Offerors shall indicate if any of the contracts listed were terminated and the type and reasons for the termination.

(3)   Section 3 New Corporate Entities

New corporate entities may submit data on prior contracts involving its officers and employees. However, in addition to the other requirements in this section, the Offeror shall discuss in detail the role performed by such persons in the prior contracts cited. Information should be included in the files described in the sections above.

(4)   Section 4 - Past Performance Assessment Questionnaire

Past performance Assessment Questionnaires must be completed and submitted for all contracts identified in Section 1. The Offeror shall complete Part I of the past performance Assessment Questionnaire and e-mail the Questionnaire to both the Government contracting activity and technical representative responsible for the past/current contract. In cases where the performance had been conducted as a subcontractor, the questionnaire shall be provided to the prime contractor POC, in addition to the Government POC. The POC's shall be instructed to electronically complete Part II of the Questionnaire and e-mail the entire Questionnaire within fifteen (15) calendar days of the release of the RFP to XXX. The Offeror shall also e-mail, to XXX, a list of all the POCs who were sent a Questionnaire. The Government must receive this list within ten (10) calendar days after release of the RFP. The POC List shall be submitted in accordance with solicitation Attachment 0003, past performance Questionnaire POC List found in Section J, Attachment 0004, of the RFP.

RFP Section M Pages 77-79:

2.   Past Performance Evaluation Approach.

The past performance evaluation will utilize relevant and recent information as it relates to this acquisition. Past performance evaluations will provide a level of expectation for the Offerors successful performance of the solicitation's requirements as indicated by that Offeror's record of past performance on relevant contracts. The Government will conduct a past performance assessment based on the two aspects of past performance: Relevancy and Confidence. In this context, Offeror refers to the proposed prime contractor and their top three major subcontractors (i.e.,the top three anticipated contract performers from a cost perspective). In each case, the prime contractor and the proposed major subcontractors will be assessed individually and the results will then be assessed in their totality to derive the Offerors past performance Confidence rating.

a.   Relevancy will be determined by those efforts related to the exploitation arena, reverse engineering, program management, testing and evaluation, prototype development and logistical support. The past performance Determination of relevancy will be based on the Offeror's and its major subcontractors' performance on Federal Government prime contracts, task/ delivery orders, and/or major subcontracts as it relates to the probability of successful accomplishment of the required effort. The examined period will encompass two (2) years from the date of issuance of the final solicitation of this effort. Areas of relevance include contracts, task/delivery orders and major subcontracts which include similarity of service/support, complexity, dollar value, contract type, and degree of subcontract/teaming to the services and supplies described in the PWS. The past performance Evaluation Team will review this past performance information and determine a relevancy rating. Each piece of past performance information will not receive an individual relevancy rating. A past performance relevancy rating will be assigned to the body of work as a whole. When assessing past performance, the Government will focus its inquiry on the past performance of the Offeror and its proposed major subcontractors as it relates to all solicitation requirements.

These requirements include all aspects of schedule, performance and supportability, including the Offerors record of: 1) conforming to specifications and standards of good workmanship; 2) adherence to contract schedules, including the administrative aspects of performance; 3) effectiveness of project management ability to quickly resolve technical problems quickly and effectively; 4) businesslike concern for the interest of its customers; 5) controlling costs and 6) performance against contract metrics in performance based contracts.

b.   Sources of past performance Information for Evaluation are as follows:

(1)   Relevant and recent past performance information shall be provided by the offeror; (2) Past performance information shall be obtained from any other sources available to the Government, to include, but not limited to: the Past Performance information Retrieval System (PPIRS), Federal Awardee Performance and Integrity Information System (FAPIIS), Electronic Subcontract Reporting Systems (eSRS), or other databases; (3) interviews with Program Managers, contracting officers, Fee Determining Officials; and (4) the Defense Contract Management Agency (DCMA).

c.   Offerors are cautioned that in conducting the past performance assessment, the Government may use data provided in the Offeror's proposal and data obtained from other sources. Since the Government may not necessarily interview or question all of the sources provided by the Offerors, it is incumbent upon the Offerors to explain the relevance of the data provided. Offerors are reminded that while the Government may elect to consider data obtained from other sources, the burden of providing past performance data rests with the Offerors.

d.   The past performance Evaluation Team will review past performance information and determine its quality and usefulness as it applies to the performance confidence assessment. Each Offeror shall be assigned a Performance Confidence Assessment rating.

B. Past Performance Factor Rating Definitions. The following rating definitions will be utilized in the evaluation of the two aspects of past performance; Relevancy and Confidence.

1.   Past Performance Relevancy Ratings

Very Relevant: Present/past performance effort involved essentially the same scope and magnitude of effort and complexities this solicitation requires.

Relevant: Present/past performance effort involved similar scope and magnitude of effort and complexities this solicitation requires.

Somewhat Relevant: Present/past performance effort involved some of the scope and magnitude of effort and complexities this solicitation requires.

Not Relevant: Present/past performance effort involved little or none of the scope and magnitude of effort and complexities this solicitation requires.

2.   Performance Confidence Assessments

Substantial Confidence: Based on the Offerors recent/relevant performance record, the Government has a high expectation that the offeror will successfully perform the required effort.

Satisfactory Confidence: Based on the Offerors recent/relevant performance record, the Government has a reasonable expectation that the offeror will successfully perform the required effort.

Limited Confidence: Based on the Offerors recent/relevant performance record, the Government has a low expectation that the offeror will successfully perform the required effort.

No Confidence: Based on the Offerors recent/relevant performance record, the Government has no expectation that the offeror will be able to successfully perform the required effort.

Unknown Confidence (Neutral): No recent/relevant performance record is available or the Offerors performance record is so sparse that no meaningful confidence assessment rating can be reasonably assigned.

RFP Past Performance Questionnaire:

PAST PERFORMANCE ASSESSMENT QUESTIONNAIRE

Please provide your candid responses. The information that you provide will be used in the awarding of federal contracts. Therefore, it is important that your information be as factual, accurate and complete as possible to preclude the need for follow-up by the evaluators. If you do not have knowledge of or experience with the company in question, please forward this Questionnaire to the person who does. Please return the completed Questionnaire within 3 days receipt. Thank you.

PART I – (To be completed by the Offeror)

A. CONTRACT IDENTIFICATION

Contractor/Company Name/Division:
Address:
Program Identification/Title:
Contract Number:
Contract Type:
Prime Contractor Name (if different from the contractor name cited above):
CAGE Code:
Contract Award Date:
Forecasted or Actual Contract Completion Date:

B. IDENTIFICATION OF OFFEROR'S REPRESENTATIVE

Nature of the Contractual Effort or Items Purchased:
Name:
Title:
Date:
Telephone Number:
FAX Number:
Address:
E-mail Address:

C. RESPONDENT IDENTIFICATION

Organization:
Name:
Title:
Date:
Telephone Number:
Address:
Fax Number:
E-mail Address:

PART II – EVALUATION (To be completed by Point of Contact – Respondent)

Exceeds Contractual Requirements (Explanation must be provided in Comments field below)
Meets Contractual Requirements
Failed to Meet Contractual Requirements (Explanation must be provided in Comments field below)

Comments:

B. Effectiveness of Project Management (to include use and control of subcontractors).

Exceptional (Explanation must be provided in Comments field below)
Satisfactory
Unsatisfactory (Explanation must be provided in Comments field below)

Comments:

C. Timeliness of Performance for Services and Product Deliverables, including the Administrative Aspects of Performance.

Exceeds Contractual Requirements (Explanation must be provided in Comments field below)
Meets Contractual Requirements
Failed to Meet Contractual Requirements (Explanation must be provided in Comments field below)

Comments:

D. Effectiveness in Forecasting and Controlling Project Cost.

Exceptional (Explanation must be provided in Comments field below)
Satisfactory
Unsatisfactory (Explanation must be provided in Comments field below)

Comments:

E. Commitment to Customer Satisfaction and Business-like Concern for its Customers' Interest.

Exceptional (Explanation must be provided in Comments field below)
Satisfactory
Unsatisfactory (Explanation must be provided in Comments field below)

Comments:

F. Overall Satisfaction.

Extremely Satisfactory (Explanation must be provided in Comments field below)
Satisfactory
Unsatisfactory (Explanation must be provided in Comments field below)

Comments:

G. General Comments. Provide any other relevant performance information.

Comments:

H. Other Information Sources. Please provide the following information:

Are you aware of other relevant past efforts by this company? If yes, please provide the name and telephone number of a point of contact:

PART III – RETURN INFORMATION

PLEASE NOTE: When completed, please send electronically via email to: XXXX

Thank you for your assistance.

Critique

The following is a critique of the past performance requirements and evaluation scheme in the example solicitation.

The past performance (PP) requirements and evaluation scheme included in the Draft RFP (DRFP) are worthy of comment in five areas: 1) How many PP citations should be submitted, 2) How PP will be evaluated, 3) How many parties receive past performance Assessment Questionnaires (PPAQs), 4) Does the evaluation scheme pass judgment on or rate how many PPAQs are returned, and 5) The form and content of the past performance Assessment Questionnaires. These areas are addressed in turn in the sections below.

How many past performance citations should be submitted

Page 71 of the DRFP states that "*offerors shall submit a list of relevant Federal Government contracts (prime contracts, task/delivery orders, and/or major subcontracts in performance during the past two years from the date of issuance of the final solicitation), which are relevant to the services and supplies required by this solicitation. Data concerning the prime Offeror shall be provided first, followed by each of the top three proposed major subcontractors (e.g.,the top three anticipated contract performers from a cost perspective), in alphabetical order."* There is no page limit on the PP volume, only a limit to 2 pages per PP. Therefore, offerors appear to be free to submit an unlimited number of PP citations.

Under these circumstances, is an offeror better off submitting only its strongest four projects (possibly the absolute minimum, for a bid team of a prime and three or more subcontractors, given the DRFP note to submit contract data for the prime and three main subcontractors), or submitting more projects to demonstrate breadth of experience? As the individual projects are not assigned a relevancy or confidence rating, this being done at the *"body of work"* level, would an offeror receive a better rating if it submitted its strongest four plus four slightly less relevant projects to show a larger *"body of work,"* or would the less relevant projects drag the offeror's overall rating down?

How past performance will be evaluated

On page 77 of the DRFP, it is stated that the Government *"will conduct a past performance assessment based on the two aspects of past performance: Relevancy and Confidence."* The DRFP goes on to describe in great detail the manner in which relevancy will be determined. Although there is a PP Confidence rating scale on page 79 of the DRFP, there is no corresponding description of how PP Confidence will be determined.

Page 78 of the DRFP states that a relevancy rating will not be assigned for each individual PP citation, rather a relevancy rating will be assigned to that *"body of work as a whole."* This language potentially leaves the offeror with less clarity than the norm of a limited number of PP citations with ratings assigned for each. A commonly encountered sequence of evaluation is that if each reference of a small number are rated as *"Very Relevant"* the whole section would be rated *"Very Relevant."* If two were only *"Relevant,"* then an offeror would expect the overall section to be rated *"Relevant."* The scheme for relevancy is explained but not this element, which would help an offeror determine how many PP citations to include. None of these things are addressed in the DRFP for rating the *"Confidence"* level of the PP citations.

How many parties receive PPAQs

On page 2 of the DRFP offerors are required to e-mail past performance Assessment Questionnaires to *"all contractual, technical, and administrative points of contact for each contract submitted in the past performance proposal. Offerors must ensure that this is accomplished in sufficient time for assessments to be completed and submitted to the contracting officer prior to the date and time set for receipt of proposals."*

On page 72 of the DRFP offerors are instructed to *"e-mail the Questionnaire to both the Government contracting activity and technical representative responsible for the past/ current contract."* When performance was as a subcontractor, offerors are to provide the PPAQ to *"the prime contractor POC, in addition to the Government POC."*

It is no secret that government parties suffer from PPQ and CPARS fatigue. Asking customers to fill out yet another round of questionnaires is an exercise in cajoling, persuading and shepherding responses through a chain of persons, many of whom feel that there are better uses of their time. Some government activities have gone so far as to issue blanket statements and policies that they will not complete PPAQs. Responding to a DRFP with the opportunity to submit an unlimited number of PP citations is an excellent opportunity for a bid team to showcase the depth and breadth of their experience over the preceding 2 years, which can be considerable. Having to persuade clients to complete a round of PPAQs diminishes the enthusiasm for this, however, which is greatly exacerbated by multiplying the number of PP citations submitted by a factor of the four or five PPAQs required for each one.

Does the evaluation scheme pass judgment on or rate how many PPAQs are returned

On page 2 of the DRFP offerors are required to e-mail past performance Assessment Questionnaires to *"all contractual, technical, and administrative points of contact for each contract submitted in the past performance proposal. Offerors must ensure that this is accomplished in sufficient time for assessments to be completed and submitted to the contracting officer prior to the date and time set for receipt of proposals."*

On page 72 of the DRFP this same point is addressed with the requirement for the Offeror to also e-mail *"a list of all the POCs who were sent a Questionnaire... within ten (10) calendar days after release of the DRFP."*

It would be imprudent to finalize a complete bid team to the point that adjustments cannot be made following RFP release and review to determine if there have been any changes to the RFP or PWS. Finalizing the bid team and making PP citation submission decisions under the 10 day requirement above means that bid teams will have precious little time to properly perform these important activities before then ensuring that PPAQs are sent out and received by the numerous parties the RFP requires to receive them and then to get a comprehensive list of same to the contracting officer. This is an unnecessarily restrictive timeline.

This sequence of activities also begs questions regarding what is being done with this information. Are the offerors being judged by the response rate of government parties to complete and return PPAQs?

Form and content of Past Performance Assessment Questionnaires

The attachment 0003 PPAQ is an MS Word document. The DRFP instructions are for offerors to e-mail these forms to POCs, who are then to fill them out and e-mail them to the contracting officer. There are three points worthy of mention regarding the form, structure and content of these PPAQs:

The structure of the questions on the PPAQ include three levels of responses for each answer. The highest and lowest *"require"* comments from the respondent. There is a clear incentive in this structure for a respondent to circle the middle rating on each and thus avoid completing free-text narratives on each question.

There have been significant advances in survey instruments over the last decade. Numerous low-cost or free survey instruments that have been validated for ease of use, survey accuracy, and respondent checking are readily available to anyone with e-mail or Internet access. Perpetuating manually intensive PPAQ response efforts that offer virtually no automation possibilities for reminders, tracking of survey completion, standardization of responses, or allowances for respondents to save work-in-progress and return to their responses compounds the response problem of getting more rather than less willingness of government officials to respond.

There is a validated expectation that multiple offers will be received in response to this solicitation. Each offeror under the current scheme has the opportunity to submit an unlimited number of PP citations, from across their team, each with an associated four or five PPAQs. These PPAQs will all be received as e-mail attachments. The burden of tracking down, organizing and evaluating this trove of PP information should be fully considered prior to continuing down this path.

Chapter 6

DISPUTES AND PROTESTS

The time may come when a firm is compelled to challenge a past performance rating or protest a decision regarding a past performance issue. As a whole, the appeals process has very specific steps and expectations for the parties involved. A well-documented appeals process is the best way to ensure that all parties' best interests are met and that an appropriate dispute resolution is reached. A firm can go about starting the dispute or protest process in various ways, present it to various venues, and obtain various outcomes based on the chosen venue. We focus on the most common scenarios.

Understanding how the government views disputes and protests over past performance issues is critical to any firm that pursues a challenge to a contract decision based on its past performance. Sample cases provide an in-depth perspective on how this information has been applied in real-life scenarios.

Three terms used in this chapter warrant additional clarity on their intended use: *venue*, *dispute*, and *protest*. We use *venue* to indicate a forum where an appeal can be made and include formal and less formal "venues" (e.g., appeal to the contracting officer) as well as the Court of Federal Claims. A *contract dispute* is defined as a "disagreement between the contractor and the contracting officer regarding the rights of the parties under a contract" (Garner, 2009). A *protest* is defined as an "objection, submitted by an interested party in writing, protesting an agency solicitation for offers, the cancellation of a solicitation, or the award or proposed award of a contract" (Nash et al., 1998).

We use *protest* and *dispute* in consonance with these definitions; however, this exacting level of definition is not always helpful. Therefore, we also use the term *disagreement* to refer to any differences in position between a contractor and the government on past performance issues, ratings, evaluations, decisions, and so on. Our use of the term includes situations that are perhaps more correctly classifiable as either a dispute or a protest.

TIMING OF DISPUTES

Past performance disagreements may arise in either of two time categories: (1) before contract award or (2) during or after contract performance. Before contract award is the period when past performance is being used as a source selection factor. The contractor is the primary source of past performance information in many cases during this period. During and after contract performance, past performance information is provided primarily by the contracting officer and representatives, not the contractor. Table 6-1 shows additional differences between disagreements arising in either of the two periods, the most significant being one of venue. In the time before award, disagreements about the use and interpretation of past performance can be heard in four possible venues. During contract performance, the primary venue for disagreements is inside the agency itself. However, CPARS and other performance evaluations can also be challenged at the Court of Federal Claims (see for example *Todd Construction v. U.S.* and *Alliant Techsystems, Inc. v. U.S.*).

Feature	Before Award	During and Following Contract Performance
Use of past performance information	Must be a source selection evaluation factor in all competitive procurements of more than $100,000 value	Must be collected on all contracts of more than $100,000 value
Primary source of past performance information	Contractor	Government officials, contracting officer, contracting officer's representative, contracting officer's technical representative
When contractor sees the evaluation	During clarifications, discussions, or debrief	"As soon as practicable," which typically means when alerted via CPARS automated email
Contractor response window	Same as protest response window if contractor alerted during debrief or award decision	Seven days to request a meeting, 14 days to comment before upload into PPIRS, 60 days to comment
Retention of past performance information	Same as other contract dispute documentation (6 years, 3 months, per FAR 4.805) in the event of a dispute	Maximum of three years after contract completion for use in source selection evaluations (FAR 42.1503).
Venues for disagreements	Contracting officer review, level above the contracting officer review, Government Accountability Office, Court of Federal Claims	Contracting officer review, level above the contracting officer review, Court of Federal Claims

Table 6-1: Impact of Pre/Postaward Timing on Past Performance Disputes

CONTRACTOR RESPONSES TO AGENCY REVIEWS DURING CONTRACT PERFORMANCE

The conclusions documented in performance assessments are decided by the contracting agency. When the initial assessment is completed by the program office, it is signed by the individual in the program who is most familiar with the contractor's performance. Then the contracting officer signs the assessment.

FAR 42.1503 allows a contractor to comment on these assessments. After the assessment is signed by all appropriate parties in the contracting office, it is sent to the contractor for comments. This should take place within 24 hours of collecting the necessary signatures. The contractor (per FAR 42.1503(d)) must be allowed a minimum of 14 days to respond to any issues raised in the assessment. When a contractor fails to provide a response by the deadline, the contracting officer should contact the contractor to encourage a written reply. If the contractor does not respond, the government's assessments stand. In either case, after 14 days, the record is uploaded into PPIRS; it is marked "pending" to indicate that agency review of contractor comments (if any) is ongoing. The assessed contractor can submit comments to the CPARS record up to 60 days after it is sent to the contractor for comment; after 14 days, the report will be available in PPIRS with or without contractor comments. At the conclusion of the 60-day period, or after the contractor comments and the agency reviews, the "pending" designation is removed.[16]

If rating disagreements arise, contractor rebuttals are first addressed by the contracting officer and the lead assessor. If they cannot resolve the disagreement, the contractor is entitled to a review from at least one level above the contracting officer. Written communication as well as a face-to-face meeting may be required. It is important to make sure that the disagreement is clearly documented and that diligent effort is put into achieving resolution. Upon completion of a government review of a contractor's comments on past performance, a copy of the completed assessment is sent by the contracting officer to the contractor.

VENUE

When entering into a disagreement process with a government agency regarding past performance, it is important to fully understand the chosen venue and to present the disagreement in the most factual and compelling manner.

---

[16] https://vsc.gsa.gov/CPARS/CPARS_Main.cfm.

Four possible venues for past performance disagreements exist: the contracting officer, the level above the contracting officer, the Government Accountability Office (GAO), and the Court of Federal Claims. Appeals to the contracting officer and appeals to a level above the contracting officer are both categorized as appeals to the agency. These venues have varied features regarding when and how they are used, time frames, standards of review, submission information, and typical outcomes (Table 6-2).

Feature	Appeal to Agency	Government Accountability Office	Court of Federal Claims
Types of appeals heard	Protests and disputes.	Protests: Written objections to a federal agency regarding the procurement of goods or services.	Protests and disputes: Alleged agency violation of a regulation or statute without any rational basis.
Reference	FAR 33	31 USC § 3551	28 USC § 1491(a)(1) and (b)(2)
Submission information	1. Detailed statement of legal and factual grounds for protest, include description of resulting prejudice to the protester. 2. Copies of relevant documents. 3. Request for a ruling by the agency. 4. Statement as to the form of relief requested. 5. All information establishing that the protester is an interested party for the purpose of filing a protest. 6. All information establishing the timeliness of the protest.	Protester must demonstrate that the government's improper action prejudiced its chance for award.	Protester must demonstrate that the government's improper action prejudiced its chance for award.

Feature	Appeal to Agency	Government Accountability Office	Court of Federal Claims
Standard of review	Subjective review with wide discretion in accordance with published or unpublished agency procedure.	Whether the procurement decision complies with statute or regulation and is consistent with the terms of the solicitation.	If the action is found to be arbitrary, capricious, an abuse of discretion, or otherwise not in accordance with law.
Level of discovery	No formal discovery process per se; FAR 33 states that "to the extent permitted by law and regulation, the parties may exchange relevant information" which is tempered by agency interpretation and action. Discovery is generally none or extremely limited. No "agency report" is required.	Limited discovery. The agency must produce the "agency report," which typically contains its official response to the protest and documents including the contemporaneous evaluation, source selection plan, and relevant correspondence, among other items.	More discovery per RCFC 26(b)(1): "Parties may obtain discovery regarding any matter, not privileged, that is relevant to the claim or defense of any party, including the existence, description, nature, custody, condition, and location of any books, documents, or other tangible things and the identity and location of persons having knowledge of any discoverable matter. For good cause, the court may order discovery of any matter relevant to the subject matter involved in the action." May under rare instances include deposition.
Time to file	Protests on solicitations: Protests on award or for other reasons or disputes: Within ten days after contract award or within five days after a debriefing date offered to the protester under a timely debriefing request.	Protests on solicitations: Before bids are due. Protests on award or for other reasons or disputes: Within ten days after basis of protest is known, or within five days after a debriefing date offered to the protester under a timely debriefing request.	Protests on solicitations: Before bids are due. Disputes or other: No specific statute of limitations applies.

Feature	Appeal to Agency	Government Accountability Office	Court of Federal Claims
Decision time frame	Best effort made to render a decision in 35 days	Within 100 days from date of filing, or within 65 days under an "express" option.	No deadline. Bid protests typically disposed of in five to six months.
Typical outcome positive for contractor	The agency may take any action or grant any remedy that could be recommended by the Comptroller General if the protest were filed with the GAO, including redoing the procurement or source selection, or recovery of costs. GAO does not hear disputes as defined here; agency has wide discretion on corrective actions for disputed PP information. Less visibility/publicity of protest. Negative decision by agency does not preclude subsequent filing of protest on same grounds to GAO.	Procurement or source selection is "done over" and protester is allowed to recover legal fees and bid and proposal costs. Fees are not recoverable if the agency takes corrective action on its own prior to issuing the agency report.	Court may award "any relief that it considers proper, including declaratory and injunctive relief." Protester allowed to recover legal fees and bid and proposal costs up to specific caps.
Typical outcome negative for contractor	Source selection or PP evaluation decision and documentation stands. No legal or other costs recovered by contractor. Risk of contractor being viewed negatively by agency and those in positions contractor routinely does business with.	Source selection decision stands. No legal or other costs recovered by contractor. Publicized protest decision and digest.	Source selection or other disputed decision stands. No legal or other costs recovered by contractor. Publicized protest decision and digest.

Table 6-2: Past Performance Protest and Dispute Venues

Appeals to the Contracting Officer

The contracting officer is the first choice of venue for any contractor who wishes to enter into a formal ratings dispute. This venue should be used after a contractor has received a past performance evaluation in which it concludes it has been given an unjust rating. It is an opportunity to voice concerns and to document facts or circumstances surrounding the evaluation that can strengthen the contractor's case for adjusting the rating.

When a contractor receives notice that a past performance rating has been documented, it has seven days in which to request a meeting with the issuer, 14 days to respond by providing comments on the report before the report is uploaded into PPIRs, and a total of 60 days to enter comments whether it has been uploaded into PPIRS or not. This response window is the same whether an evaluation is adverse, glowing, or somewhere in between. All responses must be addressed and acknowledged by the contracting officer in the CPARS form (which can be as simple as approving the report in CPARS). Agencies do not have to limit the hearing of disagreements to these periods.

When a firm submits to this venue, it is strongly advised to have well-documented evidence to support its position as well as to document attempts to have a conversation with the contracting officer to understand his or her point of view on the rating. Evidence needs to be factually based and should corroborate the contractor's response. If the rating was due to a specific individual's performance on the contractor's end, information and statements from that individual's perspective should be part of the documentation. It is in the appealing contractor's best interest to ensure that the submitted documentation supports the requested corrective action or highlights any specific actions by the firm that support its case.

The contracting officer's decision is considered final for this venue. An ideal outcome for a contracting officer venue is that the contracting officer will objectively evaluate the documentation and side with the firm during the dispute. The chances of this happening for a well-documented dispute are favorable; however, if the contracting officer does not change the contractor's past performance rating, the next step can be to appeal to the level above the contracting officer.

The principles of the FAR suggest that the contracting officer venue must be tried first: Government policy is to "resolve all contractual issues in controversy by mutual agreement at the contracting officer's level" (FAR Part 33), and to make every reasonable effort to resolve controversies prior to submitting a claim. Government agencies are also encouraged to use alternate dispute resolution procedures to the maximum extent practicable.

If what is being appealed is a CPARS rating, there is an additional dynamic to consider. When a rater changes a rating in CPARS, both the old and new ratings are retained in the report under separate tabs. However, it is unlikely that a rater will change a rating, if at all. Consider the analogy of a student disputing a grade on a (largely) subjectively graded homework assignment, such as an essay. The teacher initially assigns a grade of "F" and the student appeals. It is unlikely that the teacher will have made a tragic mistake and can be convinced to change the grade to an "A." It is much more conceivable that a teacher that initially assigns a grade of "C+" can be convinced to revise the assigned grade to a "B–." A firm considering whether to disagree with or dispute a past performance rating should consider the trade-off between the time and effort required to pursue the disagreement and the range of possible outcomes, including the likelihood that ratings will not be significantly changed and the possibility of unintended consequences with relationships in the agency the firm supports.

Appeals to a Level Above the Contracting Officer

Disagreements that cannot be resolved at the contracting officer level or receive an unsatisfactory outcome in the eyes of a contractor can be appealed at a level above the contracting officer. All documentation from the contracting officer–level appeal, along with any additional documentation the contractor wishes to include, should be presented. The agency representative's decision is considered final for this venue. Clear communication and factually accurate disputes provide the best opportunity for an optimal conclusion.

This venue takes the disagreement to a person at a higher level of authority for evaluation. The term "level above the contracting officer" is seen in various sections of the FAR, but the actual role or position of the person a contractor will work with depends on the contracting authority's organizational structure. It is important to note that the official making the decision is not appointed by the contracting officer; he or she is chosen according to the policies and procedures of the agency. Often it is the supervisor of the contracting officer or another appropriate official, who may be outside the supervisory chain. The main consideration for a contractor is whether the official is capable of making an independent review of the disagreement.

The kinds of appeals heard in this venue include both disputes and protests, as in the contracting officer venue. Appeals regarding process and procedure, application of criteria, and so on are also possibilities. There is more latitude in the contracting officer and level-above venues than in the GAO or Court of Federal Claims, which do not put themselves in the shoes of the deciding official regarding ratings assigned and limit their hearings to factual interpretations, particularly of guidelines and regulations.

Agencies have different guidelines, policies, and procedures. When submitting to this venue, it is recommended that the firm review all guidance from the agency the firm is in disagreement with, especially if this is the first time it has received an evaluation from the agency. Being informed and able to provide a detailed and accurate account of everything will strengthen the firm's position for dispute resolution in its favor.

Appeals to the Government Accountability Office

The 1984 Competition in Contracting Act provided GAO with explicit statutory authority to hear bid protests. GAO hears protests regarding whether a procurement decision complies with statute or regulation and is consistent with the terms of the solicitation. GAO will hear claims of alleged illegalities or improprieties in solicitations, cancellations of solicitations, or awards or proposed awards of contracts. GAO does not hear all issues; for example, it does not hear challenges to small business size certifications (Manuel and Schwartz, 2011).

Only those individuals or entities termed *interested parties* may have a protest decided by GAO. An interested party is an actual or prospective bidder or offeror whose direct economic interests are affected by the award of the contract or by the failure to award the contract.

When a protester submits to GAO, the burden of proving its case that the government agency violated a regulation or statue without any rational basis lies solely on its shoulders along with the assertion that the agency actions led to the individual's or entity's being discriminated against as a result. Documentation and evidence that don't clearly support this will either delay the process or stop the protest from being heard.

Resolutions and remedies recommended by GAO are considered advisory in nature and technically do not need to be enforced, because GAO is not an enforcement venue due to the "separation of powers" built into the Constitution. As an arm of Congress, GAO cannot order an executive agency to act. However, GAO's decisions are almost always followed because agencies that ignore GAO risk having their funding cut by Congress. GAO reports annually to Congress on agencies that do not follow its decisions.

If a protest filed in the GAO venue is found to have merit and is non-monetary, the resolution norm is for the GAO to recommend that the agency issue an amended solicitation, if appropriate, to address the flaws identified by GAO or otherwise redo a part of the process and award the contract in a manner which is consistent with the statute or regulation that had not previously been adhered to. If the protest resolution is monetary in nature, it is limited to costs associated with filing and pursuing the protest. This includes attorney fees, expert costs, and witness fees as well as the costs for preparing the bid and proposal.

Appeals to the Court of Federal Claims

The Court of Federal Claims venue has two bases of dispute jurisdiction:

- Deciding dispute resolutions made by interested parties under the Administrative Dispute Resolution Act (ADRA). These can be with either pre- or post-bid disagreements that have to do with violations of regulations and statues in regards to a procurement or a proposed procurement.

- Considering disputes submitted by disappointed bidders based on the Tucker Act, which provides the court with jurisdiction in claims stemming from "any express or implied contract with the United States."

The standards for review for the Court of Federal Claims venue are based on criteria in the Administrative Procedures Act. Under that act, the court must set aside any agency procurement actions found to be "arbitrary, capricious, an abuse of discretion, or otherwise not in accordance with law." These standards are satisfied when the protester provides evidence or evidence is discovered that something more than negligence alone resulted in a prejudicial outcome. Similar to the GAO venue, the disputer must clearly demonstrate that the government took deliberate improper action to prejudice an offeror's chance for an award.

Both nonmonetary and limited monetary compensations can be awarded through the Court of Federal Claims venue. Nonmonetary compensation is available only under the ADRA and includes declaratory and injunctive relief, as well as preliminary and permanent injunctions. For monetary remedies the amount is limited to the funds it would take to remedy the bid and/or the proposal preparation costs defined in the ADRA and the Tucker Act. On occasion, the prevailing party may also be entitled to collect legal costs incurred from the dispute. This was made possible for small businesses by the Equal Access to Justice Act of 1980.

BASIS OF APPEALS

If a company finds that it was given a poor evaluation by a government rater, it has choices of appeals processes to use. Government past performance ratings should have merit behind them, and if they prove to be concluded on false merits, they can be appealed and overturned, or at least required to be redone.

Problems and concerns over past performance often lead to frustration on both sides. It is challenging for the contractor as well as for the government. Being proactive, monitoring performance and relationships, and making sure that effective communication occurs are the most effective ways to prevent problems that may result in poor past performance ratings.

As a contractor, if you believe that you have taken the appropriate communication steps along the way but still find yourself facing problems due to a government rating of your past performance, you may consider taking legal action. Having well-documented files that clearly show your efforts as a contractor is a good start to building a strong case that will deliver you an optimal outcome. These actions are almost always filed against the government, not the individual who issued the evaluation. When government agency officials act in the scope of their employment, which includes preparing unbiased assessments in compliance with FAR Part 42.15, the Federal Torts Claims Act protects those individuals from legal repercussions. This means that upon certification from the Attorney General of the United States, the government will be substituted for the individual for the dispute in question.

CASE HISTORIES

Through evaluating case studies and examining the logic and reasoning of government agencies in disputes over past performance issues, contractors have qualitative comparison points to consider and can prepare stronger arguments in a dispute situation. Likewise, understanding the government's reasoning behind its decisions in disputes gives valuable insight to contractors in preparing thorough proposals and initiating or responding to any issues, disagreements, or disputes regarding past performance.

The following cases are a matter of public record. We provide only the relevant background for each case followed by questions to aid in analysis; our answers are given in Exhibit 6-A. Additional past performance–related case references appear in Exhibit 6-B. Because these cases do not have right or wrong "answers," we do not provide the historical outcomes, reasoning that (1) the historical outcomes are a matter of public record and (2) the same evidence and circumstances could be reviewed again by the same bodies with different conclusions and outcomes.

GTS Duratek, Inc. (GAO B-280511.2)

A solicitation was published by the Navy for a contract based on competitive best value source selection for the acquisition of services to reduce and dispose of radioactive waste generated by the Pearl Harbor Naval Shipyard. Source selection was to be based on two criteria:

- Offeror must meet the minimum technical requirements for project.
- The offerer who meets the minimum technical requirements for project, plus has the best past performance for the government would be awarded the job.

This indicated that *past performance was more important than price* for the job.

Three firms submitted proposals in response to the RFP and, after initial evaluations, the contracting officer reduced the field by establishing a competitive range of two: Allied Technology Group (ATG) and GTS Duratek, Inc (GTSD). The Navy was to reach its decision by evaluating each offeror's performance under existing and prior contracts for services that were the "same or similar in scope, magnitude, and complexity to the requirement." Past performance information was to be collected using five "contractor past performance data sheets;" however, the government did state that "they might contact references other than those identified by the contractor."

After conducting the past performance evaluation, Navy evaluators assigned an "excellent" rating to ATG's proposal and a "good" rating to GTSD. Since ATG also had the lower price, the Navy awarded the contract to ATG.

GTSD protested the award decision to the GAO, contending that the Navy improperly conducted a mechanistic evaluation of past performance that failed to consider a highly relevant past contract effort by GTSD. The past performance volume of GTSD's proposal discussed in detail the past contract for radioactive metal melting and recycling services. However, when GTSD submitted the five contractor past performance data sheets to the Navy, none of them cited the past contract. The dispute was based on a belief that the Navy should have considered its excellent past performance on the past contract, because that would have raised the firm's overall past performance evaluation rating and put it in line for the contract award. Additionally, the contracting officer's technical representative for the past contract was on the Navy's evaluation team and had personal knowledge of GTSD's contract performance.

The Navy contended it had no responsibility to evaluate the PHNS contract, since GTSD failed to include it in its five contractor past performance data sheets as required by the solicitation. Since GTSD had not included a data sheet for the PHNS contract, the Navy was not obligated to consider GTSD's performance on this effort in its past performance evaluation.

Questions:

1.   Based on the information above, was GTSD or the Navy correct?

2.   Does the GTSD performance on the past contract require Navy consideration even though GTSD failed to submit a contractor past performance data sheet? Why or why not?

MAC's General Contractor (GAO B-276755)

The Naval Air Station in Kingsville, Texas, issued a solicitation for an FFP contract for all materials, equipment, labor, and management necessary to accomplish interior renovations at seven units located in family housing. The solicitation stated this was a best-value competition based on the factors of price and past performance.

The agency received nine proposals for consideration in response to the solicitation. Of the nine, MAC's General Contractor bid the lowest price. In reviewing MAC's past performance, the contracting officer discovered that the company had been terminated for default on a prior janitorial contract with the Kingsville Naval Air Station. After further evaluation of the circumstances surrounding the termination, the contracting officer deemed MAC's past performance unacceptable. The project was awarded to Intra Systems despite its higher quote, because it was considered the best value to the government after past performance was factored in.

After hearing of the award to Intra Systems, MAC's protested the CO's decision to the GAO. MAC's contended that it was improper to use the termination for default in evaluating its past performance. MAC stated that it was appealing the termination for default to the United States Court of Appeals for the Federal Circuit. According to MAC's, the issues surrounding the termination were contentious and under analysis by the court. Furthermore, until the court's decision was reached, the air station should not be allowed to consider the unfavorable information in the CO's past performance evaluation.

Question:

1.   Should the Naval Air Station be allowed to review and consider past performance information on prior relevant contract issues that are under litigation by the courts? What is the rationale for your answer?

Aerospace Design & Fabrication, Inc. (GAO B-278896.2)

NASA conducted a best-value competition for administrative services to support the Lewis Research Center in Cleveland, Ohio. During the evaluation of proposals, NASA assessed a significant weakness against Aerospace Design & Fabrication (ADF) for problems it had experienced as a subcontractor on a previous contract that was relevant in size and scope to the Lewis Research Center work statement. This significant weakness had an adverse impact on the firm's past performance rating and was a major factor in its failure to win the contract.

After ADF was notified that it had not won the contract and that a weakness in its past performance was one of the key reasons for the decision, it immediately protested to the GAO. ADF claimed that the weakness in past performance was never disclosed to them during discussions as required by the FAR. The FAR, according to ADF, requires the contracting officer to disclose adverse past performance feedback and allow the contractor a chance to reply. ADF cited FAR 15.3, which states that "agencies holding discussions must permit offerors an opportunity to respond to past performance information obtained from references on which the offeror has not had a previous opportunity to comment."

NASA contended that ADF had received the opportunity to reply to this adverse report, which had come from an award fee determination briefing on another relevant contract. Under NASA policy, the contractor always receives the opportunity to submit a written response or rebuttal to a NASA award fee determination. Furthermore, it claimed that the fact that ADF was a subcontractor, not the prime contractor on the award fee determination in question, does not deny them the opportunity to reply to the adverse finding. Its subcontractor response could be forwarded to the prime contractor, which could then process it, integrate it into the prime contractor response, and forward the overall response to the government program office.

Questions:

1. Has NASA met the test of FAR 15.306 regarding communications with offerors?

2. What are the key issues in the case? What is the rationale for your answer?

3. Whom do you side with in this case, NASA or ADF?

Exhibit 6-A: Potential Answers to Case Questions

GTS Duratrek

1. Q: Based on the information above, was GTSD or the Navy correct?

    A: GTSD. GTSD makes a strong case that the Navy cannot ignore past performance information where the same scope of work under a very similar contract was observed being performed by the same activity doing the evaluation. The Navy makes a weaker case that unless the offeror explicitly provides a specific instance of past performance information in a proposal then it cannot or should not be considered.

2. Q: Does the GTSD performance on the past contract require Navy consideration even though GTSD failed to submit a contractor past performance data sheet? Why or why not?

    A: Yes, because the past performance information was "too close at hand" for the Navy to ignore. GAO review precedence is that "close at hand" information should be considered the same as any other past performance information presented by the bidder or found by the buyer.[17]

---

[17] From TRW, Inc., GAO B-282162, B-282162.2 of June 9, 1999:

While agencies generally need not evaluate all past performance references or those not reflected in the proposals, our Office has recognized that in certain limited circumstances an agency evaluating an offeror's past performance has an obligation (as opposed to the discretion) to consider "outside information" bearing on the offeror's past performance. International Bus. Sys., Inc., B-275554, Mar. 3, 1997, 97-1 CPD Para. 114 at 5. Where we have charged an agency with responsibility for considering such outside information, the record has demonstrated that the information in question was "simply too close at hand to require offerors to shoulder the inequities that spring from an agency's failure to obtain, and consider, the information." Id.; see GTS Duratek, Inc., B-280511.2, B-280511.3, Oct. 19, 1998, 98-2 CPD Para. 130 at 14 (agency should have considered offeror's performance of a prior contract where the contract was discussed in the offeror's past performance proposal, was so relevant as to have served as the basis for the government estimate for the subject solicitation, and the contracting officer's technical representative for the contract was a member of the technical evaluation team for the subject solicitation); G. Marine Diesel, B-232619.3, Aug. 3, 1989, 89-2 CPD Para. 101 at 4-6 (contracting officer that was personally aware of the

MAC's General Contractor

Q: Should the Naval Air Station be allowed to review and consider past performance information on prior relevant contract issues that are under litigation by the courts? What is the rationale for your answer?

A: When viewed from the perspective of a long-standing cultural tradition of "innocent until proven guilty," MAC's argument appears sound. However, it is disputing a subjective business decision made with the information available at the time by the government that is held to the standard of a rational decision based on adherence to the evaluation scheme delineated in the solicitation. The Naval Air Station should be allowed to consider the available information regarding the past performance information, *even if it is under litigation,* because it is making a decision independent of the findings of the potential litigation.[18]

---

awardee's continuing difficulties in performing a contract for services related to the subject solicitation, and considered the performance difficulties relevant to the extent that the contracting officer determined not to exercise the options in the contract awarded under the subject solicitation, erred in not considering the awardee's performance difficulties when determining whether the contract under the subject solicitation had been properly awarded); G. Marine Diesel; Phillyship, B-232619, B-232619.2, Jan. 27, 1989, 89-1 CPD Para. 90 at 4-5 (agency should have considered awardee's prior experience under a directly relevant contract where the contract was referenced in the awardee's proposal and the agency personnel were familiar with the awardee's performance). However, the "close at hand" information in these cases generally concerned contracts for the same services with the same procuring activity, or at least information personally known to the evaluators. See Morrison Knudsen Corp., B-280261, Sept. 9, 1998, 98-2 CPD Para. 63 at 5-6.

[18] From MAC's General Contractor, GAO B-276755 of July 24, 1997:
The termination for default clearly provides a reasonable basis for the contracting officer's concerns about the firm's past performance. See JCI Envtl. Servs., B-250752.3, Apr. 7, 1993, 93-1 CPD ¶ 299 at 7. The fact that MAC's may be appealing the ASBCA decision upholding the termination does not mean that it was unreasonable for the agency to rely on the termination as evidence of the firm's past performance; we review not whether the contracting officer's determination ultimately proves correct, but only whether it was reasonable at the time it is made. JCI Envtl. Servs., supra; see also MCI Constructors, Inc., B-240655, Nov.

Aerospace Design & Fabrication

1. Q: Has NASA met the test of FAR 15.306 regarding communications with offerors?

   A: FAR 15.306(b)(4) states that communications with offerors before establishment of the competitive range shall address adverse past performance information to which the offeror has not previously had an opportunity to comment. The implied test has two parts: whether or not the offeror is aware of the adverse past performance information and whether or not the offeror has had an opportunity to comment on it. There is no evidence presented in the case that indicates that NASA verified that ADF was aware of the adverse past performance information or had an opportunity to address it. NASA made assumptions about the firm's involvement as a subcontractor in an award fee forum that are contradictory to or outside of common practice (i.e., that a subcontractor is a direct participant in an award fee performance evaluation and feedback cycle). Under ideal conditions, a subcontractor contributing to contract performance subject to an award fee would receive feedback from the prime contractor on its performance, but there is no guarantee that this actually happened. The details of the response cycle to this feedback, including whether or not the subcontractor was able to respond to the feedback, are less certain. Therefore, NASA did not meet the test of FAR 15.306 regarding communications with offerors.

2. Q: What are the key issues in the case? What is the rationale for your answer?

   A: The key issues are whether or not NASA conducted communications as required with ADF and whether those communications affected the source selection decision. The first issue is key because it is a government requirement to have communications under these circumstances as a matter of fairness to offerors. The second issue is key because this oversight

---

27, 1990, 90-2 CPD ¶ 431 at 4; S.A.F.E. Export Corp., B-208744, Apr. 22, 1983, 83-1 CPD ¶ 437 at 2-3, aff'd, S.A.F.E. Export Corp.--Recon., B-208744.2, July 14, 1983, 83-2 CPD ¶ 90.

may have had a material impact on the outcome of the source selection.

3. Q: Whom do you side with in this case, NASA or ADF?

    A: ADF. NASA based its action to withhold communications with ADF on unreasonable assumptions about whether ADF was aware of adverse past performance information and whether it had a chance to comment or respond to it.[19]

---

[19] From Aerospace Design & Fabrication, Inc., GAO B-278896.2, B-278896.3, B-278896.4, B-278896.5 as of May 4, 1998:

...[T]estimony showed that...as a general matter, a subcontractor does not attend the award fee evaluation sessions between the agency and the prime contractor... NASA does not become involved in award fee discussions between prime contractors and subcontractors, and that a subcontractor has no opportunity to ask NASA to review the outcome of these discussions. In addition...since NASA does not attend award fee discussions between prime contractors and their subcontractors, the agency does not know the nature of the exchange between the two parties. Generally, award fee discussions may be sufficient, in some circumstances, to meet the requirements of...(the FAR regarding communications with offerors regarding adverse past performance information)...however, we do not agree that an agency can satisfy this requirement for an opportunity to comment when the award fee discussions upon which it relies were held with a different party—i.e., the prime contractor on the earlier contract, for whom ADF served as a subcontractor. We reach this conclusion based on the testimony received in this case which indicates that award fee discussions with a prime contractor—at least as conducted by NASA—do not generally afford a subcontractor any meaningful role in the exchange that is held as part of the award fee evaluation. In our view, the secondhand transmission of information from the prime contractor to the subcontractor will not normally provide the kind of opportunity for exchange and review anticipated by the requirements of (the FAR).

Exhibit 6-B: Past Performance Reference Cases

Year	Report #	Title	Key PP Areas
1998	B-278896.2; B-278896.3; B-278896.4; B-278896.5	Aerospace Design & Fabrication, Inc.	Adverse PPI and communications with offeror
2010	ASBCA No. 56940	Colonna's Shipyard, Inc.	Avoiding disputes clause with "unappealable" level above argument for CPARS
2010	B-401679.4	Shaw-Parsons; Vanguard Recovery; Joint Venture	Close-at-hand information defined and close-at-hand principle stated
1995	B-261758	Moore Medical Corp.	Close-at-hand PPI
1995	B-270518	Executive Security & Engineering Technologies, Inc.	Close-at-hand PPI
1995	B-259653.4	Maytag Aircraft Corp.	Close-at-hand PPI
1998	B-280511.2, B-280511.3	GTS Duratek, Inc.	Close-at-hand PPI
1998	B-280261	Morrison Knudsen Corp.	Close-at-hand PPI
1997	B-275554	International Bus. Sys., Inc.	Close-at-hand PPI
1989	B-232619.3	G. Marine Diesel	Close-at-hand PPI
2003	B-291402.3, B-291402.4	Phil Howrey Company	De facto debarment
2002	B-289445	Quality Trust, Inc.	De facto debarment
2000	B-286335	NMS Management, Inc.	Exchanging PPI with offerors
2000	B-286226	TLT Construction Corporation	Exchanging PPI with offerors
2000	B-284032	Universal Fabric Structures	Mergers and acquisitions
2001	B-286599	Menendez-Donnell & Associates	No relevant past performance
2000	B-284684, B-284684.2	Hydraulics International, Inc.,	No relevant past performance
2000	B-286326	Sterling Services, Inc.	Pass/fail strategies
2001	B-286597.3, B-286597.4, B-286597.5, B-286597.6,	OSI Collection Services, Inc.; C.B. Accounts, Inc.	Past performance evaluation process

Year	Report #	Title	Key PP Areas
2000	B-285651	North American Aerodynamics, Inc.	Past performance evaluation process
2001	B-287325	Oceaneering Intl Inc.	Past performance versus experience
2001	B-288655	Goode Constr. Inc.	Past performance versus responsibility determinations
2000	B-284240	PEMCO World Air Services	Performance assessment reports
2003	B-291507, B-291507.2	Kira, Inc.; All Star Maintenance, Inc.	PPI currency
2001	B-285358	Symtech Corp.	PPI relevancy
1997	B-276755	MAC's General Contractor	PPI under litigation
1990	B-240655	MCI Constructors, Inc.	PPI under litigation
1983	B-208744	S.A.F.E. Export Corp.	PPI under litigation
1983	B-208744.2	S.A.F.E. Export Corp.--Recon.	PPI under litigation
2000	B-284116	Champion Service Corporation	Proposal risk versus performance risk
1989	B-236028	Questech, Inc.,	Proposal risk versus performance risk
1994	B-257294	Cleveland Telecommunications Corp.	Subcontractor performance
1995	B-262051	Fluor Daniel, Inc.	Subcontractor performance
1995	B-260968.2	TRW, Inc.	Subcontractor performance

Notes. PP = past performance; PPI = past performance information.

Chapter 7

THE CHANGING FACE OF PAST PERFORMANCE

- →

The collection and use of past performance information by the government continues to be refined and improved. Ensuring success with past performance requires staying abreast of and understanding the causes and directions of these changes. This chapter is about what has caused and will cause the use of past performance to change and how it is currently changing. Also included in this chapter are examinations of what can be learned from other exemplars, including interest groups, industry associations, commercial buyers, and others.

WHAT CAUSED PAST PERFORMANCE TO RISE IN IMPORTANCE?

Initially, past performance information on prospective sellers was viewed by government buyers as a way to evaluate the future performance of a seller. Stemming from this initial reason is the concern that the large government buyer will unknowingly continue to award contracts to underperforming sellers. As with many systems of information collection and retention, the initial purpose the system was established to perform was not easily achieved. Fully achieving the original purpose has proceeded down a long, difficult path. Along the way, as more interactions occurred with the system, additional uses were identified, and remain to be incorporated, and additional, yet similar, purposes that could be served were folded in. An example of this is the current effort to completely integrate modules on architect and engineering (ACASS) and construction contracts (CCASS) into the CPARS system. Another example is found in government activities using CPARS reports in lieu of past performance questionnaires in solicitation responses and proposal evaluations.

WHAT WILL CAUSE IT TO CHANGE?

What has most recently caused the collection, retention, and use of past performance information to change has been a prolonged period of activity intended to address shortcomings between the potential utility of the government system and the (lower) current utility derived from the system. The pace of systematic government improvements has accelerated, and changes have focused on compliance by agencies and activities with collecting and fully documenting past performance information. Additionally, improvement efforts have focused on increasing the accessibility of collected information and increasing the breadth of information collected, as is the case with the System for Award Management and the recent collection and retention of bio-preferred information in this system intended to increase federal procurement of bio-based products.

The overall ecosystem around past performance in the government contracting market, including the aggregate of behaviors, methods, and norms that comprise the commonalities of collection, evaluation, retention, and use of past performance information across the government contracting market, is a complex, adaptive system. This system has elements of both an organization, where planned changes could be imposed upon the system, and an open system, where innovations originate or emanate from experiments that move parts of the system away from normal routines, intricate networks connect interdependent subsystems to one another, micro-level diversity supplies seeds of novelty, innovations confer new functionalities that enhance adaptability to unexpected changes or jolts from the environment, and critical periods of instability allow substantive transformation of behaviors and dynamics (Goldstein et al., 2010).

In plainer language, the impetus behind changes to this system seem to come through several familiar pathways: (1) through grassroots efforts, (2) through the actions of elected representatives to address specific issues or constituencies, and (3) in response to management by fiat. Figure 7-1 shows an illustrative next level of detail on the steps that compose each of these pathways.

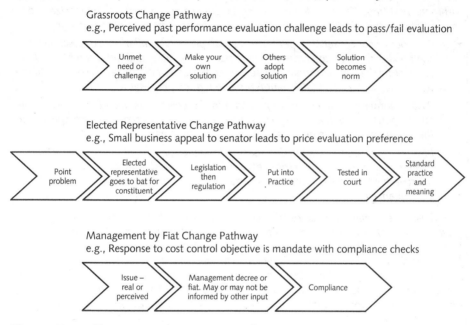

Figure 7-1: Change Pathway Examples

A *grassroots effort* refers to where a localized solution is used to address a need or challenge that is otherwise not addressed. The localized solution gains traction through use and refinement. The use of the localized solution may spread to other places and users by word of mouth or through other means of dissemination. At some point, what started as a localized solution becomes officially or unofficially more widely adopted and is perhaps codified in some way. Of note here is that a localized solution may be nothing more than an expediency, or to put a finer point on it, a way to make life easier "in the trenches" without regard for broader implications of systematically using the expedient to get things done. An example of this is the use of pass/fail past performance evaluation schemes like those currently being used in several Department of Homeland Security components. Rather than go through the effort to fully evaluate and discretely grade past performance as part of source selection, a pass/fail scheme is used as shown in Figure 7-2.

PAST PERFORMANCE (Volume I)

The Offeror's past performance will be evaluated based on an assessment of work performed within the past three (3) years demonstrating experience on contracts of similar size, scope and complexity specifically experience in the areas of (specific type of) engineering.

- *Past performance reflects performance on projects similar in size, scope, and complexity to the requirements contained in the RFP and attachments. (While conducting the past performance assessment, the Government may use data obtained from other sources and information provided in the proposal.)*

- *Past performance references are current and the degree to which the Offeror's role and responsibilities under the projects are similar in size, scope and complexity to the requirements contained in the RFP and attachments*

- *Past performance reflects the Offeror's performance and client support to include quality of services, delivery/completion of products, cost control, systemic improvements, and small business utilization and subcontracting goals during the performance period*

The Government may contact references cited by the Offeror in their proposal. The Government may obtain additional information on past performance from other sources such as Government past performance databases, Inspector General reports, and the Government Accountability Office reports. The information presented in the Offeror's proposal, together with information from any other sources available to the Government, will provide the primary input for evaluation of this factor. The Government reserves the right to verify the specifics of current or previous contracts described by the Offeror's proposal.

Evaluation of past performance will allow the Government to determine whether the Offeror consistently delivered quality services in a timely manner. The Offeror's past performance will be evaluated based on an assessment of work performed within the past three (3) years providing services on contracts of similar size, scope, and complexity, specifically experience in the areas of information systems integration.

In general, past performance will be evaluated by assessing the relevancy and quality of work performed in accordance with the criteria described above in this section. Additionally, the Offeror will be evaluated on client satisfaction with the previous performance of the Offeror; the Offeror's effectiveness in managing and directing resources; the Offeror's demonstration of reasonable and cooperative behavior in dealing with clients; the Offeror's quality of previously performed services; the Offeror's ability to control costs and manage contract activities; and meeting schedules in providing services and products.

In the case of an Offeror without a record of relevant past performance or for whom information on past performance is not available, the Offeror may not be evaluated favorably or unfavorably on past performance.

The following adjectival ratings will be used to score the Offeror's past performance. The adjectives and corresponding definitions are given in the table below.

Rating System for Evaluation of Past Performance Factors	
Rating	Definition
Acceptable (A)	Very little risk anticipated with delivery of quality products, on time, or of degradation of performance of lack of customer satisfaction (or cost growth if applicable) based upon the Offeror's past performance.
Neutral (N)	No relevant past performance available for evaluation. Offeror has asserted that it has no relevant directly related or similar past performance experience. Proposal received no merit or demerit for this factor.
Unacceptable (U)	Significant risk anticipated with delivery of quality products, on time, and of degradation of performance based upon the Offeror's past performance. A rating of unacceptable does not itself make the proposal ineligible for award.

Figure 7-2: Pass/Fail Past Performance Evaluation Scheme

From 2013 DHS Component RFP (competitive procurement for engineering services over $100 million).

"Through the actions of elected representatives" refers to a cycle where an issue is brought to the attention of an elected official, typically by a party or parties that are or perceive themselves to be unfairly treated. It does not have to be an aggrieved party that highlights the issue; it could as easily be a committee formed or otherwise dedicated to examining a specific issue or set of circumstances that then puts forth a call for action in some form. The office of the elected representative takes up the cause of the aggrieved and champions legislation to address the issue. The enacted law eventually makes its way into regulation. At this point, the regulation is put into practice by people who interpret and act on the regulation. Inevitably, disputes occur, which are taken up by a court or other resolution forum. Over time, this cycle of enactment, interpretation, use, testing, and dispute resolution provides standard meaning and principles.

An example of this is the (FAR 19.1307) price evaluation preference for historically underutilized business zone (HUBZone) small business concerns. Based on concerns raised in meetings with small businesses regarding receiving training but not work or contracts, in the 1990s, Senator Kit Bond championed legislation aimed at fostering the growth and livelihood of federal HUBZone contractors to empower communities, create jobs, and attract private investment. The HUBZone Empowerment Contracting program was enacted through provisions in the Small Business Reauthorization Act of 1997. Public comments were sought by the Small Business Administration on a proposed rule to implement the laws published in 1997, and the final rule for the HUBZone Empowerment Contracting Program was published in June 1998 (see 63 *CFR* 31896) with final FAR language published in September 1999 (see 64 *CFR* 51830). The new FAR language included provisions to add a factor of ten percent to the base offer price of all offers except small businesses and HUBZone small businesses during a price competition under certain circumstances. These FAR provisions have been used during proposal evaluations and source selections and have been repeatedly visited during dispute resolutions. For example, GAO's decision (GAO B-404952[20]) on an award protest by Explo Systems, Inc., describes in detail the correct application of the HUBZone price preference in response to an agency's argument for not applying the price preference in a best-value trade-off source selection process. Over time, the examination of the basis for disputes and subsequent published findings regarding the application of law and regulation has served to established standard meaning and interpretations for these provisions.

In response to management by fiat means that a level of management, with authority to do so, decrees that it shall be done thusly. Activities and the people in them are then compelled to comply with the decree. An example of this is the Under Secretary of Defense's "Should Cost" memo directed to defense acquisition managers (2013). This memo references one of the tenets of the Department of Defense's (DoD's) Better Buying Power initiative and dictates that specific actions be taken to implement should cost measures on Acquisition Category I, IA, II, and III programs. Language in the memo is directive, naming specific parties responsible, what they will do, and how compliance with the mandate will be monitored.

---

[20] www.gao.gov/assets/400/392546.pdf.

ARE THERE MODELS TO LEARN FROM?

As changes are proposed, it is natural to consider the options, including examining the pros and cons of alternative courses of action. An extension of this is to ask, Are there models or patterns worthy of replicating or putting to use? Conversely, it is useful to be able to recognize ideas, actions, or policies that have been proven worthless.

Specific Disciplines or Interest Groups

Other interest groups and associations provide limited insight into how buyers outside the government consider and treat past performance when purchasing supplies and services. The Institute for Supply Management[21] advocates an evaluation of suppliers based on their work that includes objective criteria such as financial stability or safety records as well as subjective assessments of such things as past performance. There is a distinct emphasis on financial stability along with calls to examine the credibility of the potential supplier in its industry. Additionally, the potential supplier's network and how it is supported by it are promoted as information to consider when contemplating a business relation with a source of supply.

Similarly, the principles of the supply chain management discipline tell buyers to closely examine the financial stability and capacity of potential suppliers to help determine a supplier's ability to perform. The Council of Supply Chain Management Professionals (CSCMP) underscores the importance of performing robust due diligence on potential suppliers, citing evidence of the supply chain's potential for high impact on a company's valuation (Tate, 2013). CSCMP notes that companies with well-run supply chains outperform other companies and that supply chain issues can rapidly demolish a firm's good standing with stakeholders, stockholders, and the general public. Supply chain management advocates also promote and pursue collaboration with suppliers and highlight the need for firms to ensure that potential suppliers' motivations, collaboration style, vision, and values align with those of the buying firm.

---

[21] www.ism.com.

Another industry group, The Sustainability Consortium, promotes the use of key performance indicators to assess and track suppliers' sustainability performance relative to other suppliers. These indicators are sets of questions that focus on environmental and social issues related to a specific category of goods according to a research-based "sustainability profile."[22] For example, the firm Marks and Spencer, a well-known multinational retailer headquartered in London, specializes in clothing and luxury food products. Its managers use the key indicators the Consortium has developed for these categories to evaluate suppliers before acceptance and during performance against the criteria in the appropriate sustainability profiles.

Large Buyers in Other Industries

Large buyers in other industries tend to focus supplier evaluation and monitoring programs on criteria that are critical to their core and differentiating competitive competencies. For example, retailers such as Target, Best Buy, Office Depot, Office Max, Staples, and Walmart all have vendor compliance programs used to judge suppliers and hold them responsible for quality and on-time delivery.

Walmart has more than $473 billion in revenue and has committed to sourcing an additional $250 billion from American suppliers over the next ten years (Walmart, 2014). When Walmart focuses on a certain initiative, its influence is pervasive. Walmart considers its supplier management program to be a competitive advantage and runs a tightly scripted vendor acceptance program that includes an emphasis on participation by small businesses designated as minority- or woman-owned. Walmart buyers look at Dun and Bradstreet reports on potential vendors and do not accept suppliers with risk ratings of seven or above in the financial assessment section (where a score of one indicates low risk and nine reflects the highest risk). Walmart also starts new suppliers out in a local market as part of its ongoing evaluation of the vendor before relying on them for nationwide distribution. Walmart looks for vendors with broad non-Walmart experience by accepting only suppliers able to show that

---

[22] www.sustainabilityconsortium.org/our-products.

75 percent or more of their business comes from entities other than Walmart. Walmart provides its suppliers with specific feedback, providing numerically ranked scorings of shipments to Walmart, including the vendor's ranking against other vendors in the same product categories. A given supplier can see its ranking against a competitive grouping but cannot see the rankings of its competitors. In addition to the ranking and scoring provided, Walmart provides its suppliers with improvement steps. Improvement steps make use of the Category Sustainability Profiles discussed in the preceding section, such as the percentage of responsibility-sourced palm oil for food or personal care products and the percentage of product revenue for laundry detergent that includes educational messages about the environmental benefits of washing in cold water. Walmart promotes five elements of successful supplier score carding: management buy-in, supplier incentives (primarily financial), training tools and support, integrating the scorecard program into existing business processes, and celebrating successes. Suppliers who score well are recognized and rewarded by Walmart. Suppliers who don't perform well have management meetings scheduled with Walmart to jointly develop improvement plans, and they are dropped if they do not improve (Roberts and Berg, 2012).

The primary lesson from these examples is to base supplier selection on criteria that are critical to the buyer's core competency or competencies that form the basis of its competitive advantage. Competitive advantage may conceivably be translated into "mission" for government agencies as buyers. A secondary lesson is to consider high-stakeholder interest areas in supplier selection, e.g., sustainability attributes or environmental and social concerns.

HOW DO SUCCESSFUL FIRMS MANAGE THEIR PAST PERFORMANCE?

Successful government contracting firms are fully aware of and engaged in the management of past performance information and reputation. Five specific activities they engage in are (1) proactively managing past performance and associated information, (2) gaining insights through an objective customer satisfaction program, (3) proactively engaging with clients who complete or could complete CPARS or other performance reports, (4) applying knowledge management principles to managing and extracting value from their past performance information, and (5) using past performance and customer satisfaction inputs to improve operations and performance, further enhancing their reputations in the marketplace.

Proactively Managing Past Performance and Associated Information

Successful firms nurture and develop their past performance information. They maintain libraries of searchable and readily accessible past performance information that is continuously refined and utilized in a variety of formats and for varied purposes including in proposals, in marketing campaigns, and in educating new members of the organization about firm capabilities. Leading firms are aware of and act on developing and using the different levels of past performance stories (see Chapter 3).

Objective Customer Satisfaction Programs

Successful firms have an objective customer satisfaction program, where the firm is able to appropriately administer the program. Reliance on the CPARS system and feedback loop as the sole source of customer satisfaction is not enough to satisfy seekers of objective customer satisfaction information. Appropriately administering in this context does not mean being able to manipulate what is said by whom about company past performance, but simply that the firm shapes the program and does what it can to solicit and receive honest feedback on perceptions of its performance. It also means that the firm is able to construct, refine, and evolve the methods and questions and channels used to solicit and receive feedback that can be used for a variety of purposes including (1) obtaining customer testimonials for marketing or other campaigns, (2) identifying customer champions for existing or new work, (3) improving performance, and (4) gauging differences in perceptions of firm performance and how to improve these perceptions at all levels in a client's organization.

Active CPARS Management

Successful firms are fully engaged in active CPARS management. An example of an active CPARS management approach that includes the elements of an effective program is included in Chapter 4. This active management is used to ensure that there are no surprises to the firm on completed CPARS and other forms of customer feedback, including past performance questionnaires. It is also executed to facilitate timely completion of CPARS and other performance documentation, to ensure that the firm's voice is heard in the performance reports, and to tell a complete story when performance is documented.

Applying Knowledge Management Principles to Past Performance Information

Successful firms apply knowledge management principles to past performance information, including the tenets of capturing, developing, sharing, and making effective use of company knowledge. Successful firms do not claim expertise at the use of knowledge management enabling tools—they demonstrate proficiency through active use of these tools. At these firms, past performance information is catalogued and archived and is completely searchable by all members of the organization. Intuitive systems and processes are in place that enable organizational members to quickly search, locate, and access relevant performance information regardless of the immediate use: writing a proposal section, tailoring a client or prospective client briefing, or archiving freshly developed or newly captured performance information.

Using Past Performance and Customer Satisfaction Inputs to Improve Performance and Operations

Successful firms are not solely reactive and singularly reliant on someone else (a client) deciding when, where, and how to provide past performance information. Nor do they receive this type of information only to "file and forget" it. Instead, they seek out and facilitate information and perceptions on their performance from multiple current and prospective customers, teammates, and employees.

A distinguishing characteristic of a successful firm in this arena is *what happens next*—namely, that the information received is appropriately and thoughtfully considered, ensuring no undue filtration (e.g., by the project manager whose bonus is tied to performance), followed by taking action on the information received. Actions may include deciding to not use that client for a past performance reference on future bids, changing how something specific is accomplished on the project under evaluation, or using the knowledge gained to showcase for the client how additional firm capabilities can be applied to help them with challenges that may be outside the scope of the current project.

WHAT ARE GOVERNMENT BUYERS AND POLICYMAKERS DOING?

The last time there was a significant level of activity was 2002, when DoD endorsed the Past Performance Information Retrieval System (PPIRS) as the single authorized application for retrieving contractor performance information, followed by its 2004 designation of CPARS as the DoD solution for collecting contractor performance information. In 2014, there is a renewed emphasis on past performance, which stems in part from a prolonged inability of the government to realize the intended benefits of collecting past performance information. Thus the primary activity is questioning current practices, along with improving the inputs and uses of the current system of past performance information collection and retention.

Questioning Current Practices

Government practices and outcomes associated with past performance have been criticized for a long time. Combined with a recognition among program managers, contracting officers, and policymakers that the current way of doing business has shortcomings that must be overcome for its utility to increase, these criticisms have prompted the questioning of current practices. Three common strategies can be seen at work in agency responses: examining current practice and how it could be improved, figuring out ways to work with or around the systems and processes in place, and living with the status quo.

Only a few agencies have studied making current practice more effective at a high enough or central enough level to impact policy and thus practice. Some agency-level (e.g., GSA) and policy-level (e.g., OFPP) studies have sought outside viewpoints and included industry groups in their efforts to understand how to improve collection and use. But these studies have not been conducted on a global or enterprise scale, nor have they examined in a disciplined manner the fundamental question: Is it worth it? Is there value in conducting and archiving past performance evaluations? Taking the benefits of a process or system as a given is the norm, but it undermines the credibility of any analysis to proceed from this assumption. Most examinations of current practice are compliance-oriented, do not question the status quo, and thus limit themselves to recommendations meant to enforce compliance with current processes and procedures.

In some instances, programs and contracting offices have questioned the value of the systems or processes in place and have taken steps toward figuring out something that works for their circumstances. This is not a small step for an agency or for the parties responsible for doing it. To do this openly requires a willingness to be noted as sidestepping or working around current processes. Examples of this are the NASA Solutions for Enterprise Wide Procurement program's posting of contractor performance as noted in the below section on accessibility, and the use of a pass/fail past performance evaluation scheme as discussed earlier in this chapter.

Living with the status quo, or taking the path of least resistance, is the approach of most agencies. Here, the response is essentially to note that current practices are less than ideal and then do nothing substantive about them. This pathway naturally perpetuates current practice, complete with all the shortcomings observed in this book, and makes no worthwhile impact.

Improving the Current System

During the past decade, agencies and policy makers have tried to improve and to increase compliance with past performance reporting requirements. GAO noted in 2013 that the percentage of completed *required* DoD past performance evaluations increased from 56 to 74 percent from October 2011 to April 2013, the *total number* of past performance evaluations completed increased by a factor of two between 2010 and 2012, and the number of past performance evaluations completed *on time* increased from approximately 5,600 to 14,000 between 2010 and 2012 (GAO, 2013). DoD leaders attributed these compliance improvements to an increased ability to track completed evaluations as well as to a doubling of the number of personnel trained in completing them.

In 2013, several non-DoD government agencies focused on improving the inputs to and use of the current system. One agency's efforts have focused on ensuring that (1) required CPARS reports are completed, (2) the content entered into CPARS is more than perfunctory (i.e., there is enough of a narrative entered to support the ratings assigned), and (3) ratings are not inflated. One agency developed a rubric based on the 2013 FAR Part 42 rewrite that is to be used by contracting officer representatives as a guide to completing these performance assessment reports.

The role of the contracting officer's representative typically requires various forms of program or project management experience. People assigned to these roles frequently come from elements of the customer organization responsible for program management. The contracting officer, as the approver of CPARS reports, relies on the contracting officer's representative and program management to provide the content and evaluation ratings for these performance assessments. Management efforts to improve the inputs to the current system usually focus on these roles. The most visible users of past performance information systems are contracting officers and contract specialists. There is thus a divide of sorts between those typically attempting to use what is in a past performance information system (i.e., contracting officers) and those with the responsibility to enter information into the system (i.e., program managers). Challenges with this division of labor stem from the dynamic of the contracting officer community lamenting and exhorting the efforts of the program management community to populate information in systems where the program management community is not as quick to recognize the need for this information as readily as the contracting officer community.

Exploring Ways to Increase Accessibility

Increasing accessibility to past performance information is an area of interest to buyers and sellers alike. Government agencies have expressed a belief that increased access and visibility can be used to incentivize and improve contractor performance. For example, the Navy is making headlines with its Superior Supplier Incentive Program, which names superior suppliers based on their performance on contracts, based in part on three years of CPARS information. The Navy uses this program to incentivize these and other contractors to improve performance in exchange for benefits such as public recognition and relaxing of certain contract requirements. Sellers have expressed interest in being able to see other contractors' ratings to make teaming or subcontracting decisions. Public comments on proposed FAR rule changes in 2013 have included the idea that allowing firms to see each other's ratings on subcontractor management will help them determine who is a better prime contractor relative to payment cycle times and sharing of work with subcontractors.

An example of increasing accessibility, at least to top-line rating information, is the NASA Solutions for Enterprise Wide Procurement program's posting of contractor performance information on a public web page.[23] This program has figured out an effective way to increase transparency and put some teeth into holding contractors accountable for performance on a specific contract. The program is careful to label the posted contractor ratings as "current performance" versus "past performance" to avoid directly contradicting OFPP guidance that CPARS is the system that must be used to collect and document contractor past performance information.

---

[23] www.sewp.nasa.gov/past_perf.shtml.

Exploring the Use of End User/Mass Reviews

Government policymakers have taken note of the proliferation of end user or mass reviews in some Internet-centered companies' business practices, whether via "five-star" rating schemes or substantive comments. At least one agency (the Small Business Administration) has expressed interest in this, and a request for information has been drafted to solicit input from industry on how the use of such a system to provide ratings of small businesses could benefit buyers and sellers. This is a fledgling effort that as of 2014 has not been fully explored but that we note here as an example of an innovation at least one agency is interested in discovering more about.

Shortening Cycle Times

In August 2013, the FAR Council published a proposed rule (FAR Case 2012-028) to shorten the period of time contractors had to respond to or comment on their past performance evaluations from 30 to 14 days before CPARs migrate into PPIRS. This proposed rule implements Section 806 of the 2012 National Defense Authorization Act and Section 853 of the 2013 National Defense Authorization Act. The proposed rule provides revised FAR 42.1503 language specifying the 14-day response time. The stated purpose behind this proposed change is to ensure that "timely, accurate, and complete information on contractor performance is included in past performance databases used for making source selection decisions."[24] Additionally, the proposed change allows contractor comments to be added to the past performance evaluation *after* the evaluation has been stored in PPIRS.

The public comment period closed on this proposed rule in October 2013, and the government collected ten comments. With one exception, the comments received all disagreed with shortening the contractor comment period. A number of valid points were raised in these comments:

---

[24] National Defense Authorization Act for Fiscal Year 2012. H. R. 1540 Rep. No. 112-329, at 664.

- Posted past performance evaluations would not reflect contractor comments to be entered later, and source selection officials could base decisions on incomplete or inaccurate information.

- The already difficult task of coordinating a CPAR review by a firm, including fact checking and responding across large and global enterprises, will become nearly impossible within the 14-day period.

- Allowing source selection officials access to partially completed records (i.e., allowing contractor comments and further associated revisions to a record to be added or entered after the evaluation has been placed in PPIRs) will increase (1) the number of disputes and (2) the number of decisions made on incomplete information.

This proposed change has subsequently been implemented and highlights that efforts are under way to shorten the cycle time between contract performance and a record of the evaluation of that performance becoming available for use by others. Unfortunately, this change focused on one of the shortest segments in the cycle and places the burden unfairly on the firm whose performance is being evaluated and recorded. The longer and less-enforced portions of the cycle allotted for evaluations to be completed and posted are disregarded. As recently as April 2013, the GAO noted that "more than half of federal agencies had no required contractor assessments in PPIRS." This report also notes that DoD "received comments from contractors on over 80 percent of all assessments from FY 2010 through 2012, and most were received within the [then-]current 30-day minimum requirement for responding" (GAO, 2013).

Although shortening allowable times for contractor comments before PPIRS posting is widely considered to be a lopsided treatment of the past performance cycle, it is another example of an effort to shorten the past performance cycle.

Chapter 8

THE FUTURE OF PAST PERFORMANCE

-------- ➔

We began our journey by providing a look back into the origination of the use of past performance by the government as a buyer and its early history. We conclude with a discussion of the future of past performance.

What will past performance look like in the future? The collection and use of past performance information by the government continues to be refined and improved, albeit more slowly than many would like. Trends that have originated in other markets will be explored by government users and policymakers. Thoughtful application of these ideas will be tried and adapted for use by government buyers and program managers. These include shortened feedback times, improved identity management, more parties able to contribute to past performance reviews, and increased accessibility of information, increasing the utility of the whole exercise of collecting and archiving past performance information. The following sections describe ten trends most likely to be witnessed in the relatively near future as the government's collection and use of past performance information continues to evolve.

SHORTER CYCLE TIMES

The physical capability to reduce the time between information origination and posting (where others can access it) to zero already exists even if not completely in place in government past performance systems. Pressures to increase the use of and utility obtained from past performance information repositories, combined with highlighted agency metrics on timeliness and completeness of recording past performance information will continue to provide an impetus to reduce cycle time. Cycle time is a relatively simple concept and also relatively easy to improve. Thus, in spite of calls for prudence, objectivity, and thorough review that emphasize quality over quantity or speed, cycle times will continue to be a focus of reduction efforts.

INCREASED STANDARDIZATION AND DIGITIZATION

Standardization of past performance information is already occurring, as shown by the 2013 FAR Part 42 rewrite, which standardized the documentation and evaluation of contractor performance. Another example is the roll-up of CCASS, ACASS, and FAPIIS into CPARS, all intake systems for PPIRS. These mergers highlight instances of the collection and storage of similar or duplicate information. Additional standardization across agencies and repositories will occur.

But the current non-standard system of past performance questionnaire (PPQ) use is long overdue for reform. Government agencies currently rely on all manner of extremely unsophisticated and labor-intensive PPQ submission formats. Many of the formats in use today require handwritten responses into non-standardized and non–machine-readable formats. In most cases these are received via e-mail, but they are also hand-delivered or snail-mailed. Standardization and elimination of non-digitized methods will increase along with the not-yet-begun incorporation of PPQ data into past performance information repositories.

In addition, the content of past performance questionnaires can and should be tailored to the intended use—but may or may not be, depending on the agency and contracting official overseeing their use. This component of the evaluation and use of past performance information is long overdue for improvement.

One improvement that has occurred in small ways is the standardization of questionnaires. Non-standardization was noted earlier as contributing to the phenomenon of PPQ fatigue, in which a frequent bidder on government projects has to repeatedly ask its clients to fill out and submit various permutations of PPQs on accelerated timelines to support its bids. In 2011, the U.S. Army Corps of Engineers and the Naval Facilities Engineering Command put in place a standardized PPQ process and form. The standardized process has contractors submitting completed PPQs with proposals, requesting PPQs from clients at the completion of each project, and retaining these PPQs for use in future proposal submissions. The standardization also uses the same adjectival rating scheme and factors as found in CPARS. Standardization as done by the Naval Facilities Engineering Command and the U.S. Army Corps of Engineers reduces the potential for PPQ fatigue but also appears to replicate some of the main elements of CPARS reporting (specifically CCASS and ACASS) and place the burden of collection, retention, access, and distribution on the contractor.

INCREASED ANALYZABILITY OF INFORMATION IN REPOSITORIES

Currently, information in past performance repositories is not uniform enough to robustly data-mine and analyze. As standardization and digitization continue to increase, analyzability of past performance information will improve, leading to increased transparency and creating an accelerating and self-reinforcing cycle of transformation of information repositories.

MORE ROBUST REVIEWER IDENTITY

Angie's List (www.angieslist.com) provides a well-known repository of end user reviews. As summarized in its "reviews you can trust" tagline, it believes that reviews you can trust "come from real people like you, not anonymous users." The element of being able to understand and validate a reviewer's identity and to associate this with the quality of any given review is largely absent from government systems. The identity of the contracting officer associated with a review typically can be found, but the more detailed and highly relevant information for seriously considering the merit of a reviewer generally cannot be found, such as:

- What is the vantage point of the reviewer—end user, management chain of the end user, or providing business support to the line unit that actually used the item or service?

- What is the scoring norm of the reviewer? Is the 8 out of 10 score high for that reviewer or is it low for that reviewer?

- What were the reviewer's motivations at the time of delivery of the product or service—constrained by budget and seeking lowest acceptable performance? *Not* constrained by budget and in search of *highest* possible performance?

As transparency and access increase, examination of who the reviewers are and the part that reviewer identity and accountability play in how past performance evaluation information is perceived and used by others will continue.

INCREASED REVIEWER ACCOUNTABILITY

Closely associated with the increased understanding of the identity of the reviewer is accountability of the reviewer. With increased reviewer transparency will come a corresponding rise in accountability. Examples of increased accountability can be found in the Amazon and eBay user communities. Amazon reviewers with one review of a friend's book or other product are viewed skeptically by the community. In other instances, people have become valued sources of product review information and provide thorough reviews consistently on large numbers of items found on Amazon. Additionally, Amazon asks readers of reviews to rate the usefulness of each review. Similarly, members (both buyers and sellers) of the eBay community are greatly affected by their user ratings, which are short, free-text narratives plus number of star ratings about their performance during previous transactions. Negative or few ratings can make it difficult for members with these attributes to be taken seriously and to be trusted by other members of the community. In 2012, a similar "was this information useful" input was added to PPIRS. Full use of this added functionality and the effects of its use are still to be seen and understood.

INCREASED ACCESS TO INFORMATION

Accessibility of past performance information and analysis, including an expansion of viewpoints included, will increase in the future. Increased accessibility of information does not just mean that what some gatekeeper allows to be entered into a system is more widely available; it also means that more real-time, unfiltered information will become available. An example is the trend and power in most mass review systems of note where anyone can add to the review discussion/comment chain, and what is added can be seen in real time, including the perspective of the seller. We are currently far away from contractor and government comments in real time in CPARS/ PPIRS, but are on a trend that includes this element.

An exemplar of how this can work and improve government-industry interaction is being used today by the U.S. Army on its acquisition portal, Army Single Face to Industry,[25] and by the U.S. Navy on its SeaPort contract portal.[26] During the time a competitive procurement is announced and solicited, interested parties can submit questions that post to the respective site in real time. When the government provides answers, these are also posted in real time for all to see. Although a government respondent (typically a contracting officer or contract specialist) could wait to post answers until all of the answers are assembled, what more frequently occurs—and which is the intent of these portals—is that answers are posted as they are formulated. In this way, both sides of the conversation (buyers and sellers) can see what questions have been asked, the answers, and whether answers have been posted. This is not the same as real-time conversation, but it is a huge improvement over submitting questions

---

[25] https://acquisition.army.mil/asfi.

[26] www.seaport.navy.mil.

without the benefit of seeing any other users' questions and waiting in prolonged anticipation for the government to issue responses— which are typically delayed while one or two questions that hold up any answers being released are staffed and answered.

BROADER PARTICIPATION IN REVIEWS

Several trends noted here will lead to the inclusion of more parties having contributory access to past performance information repositories. As the accountability of the reviewer and the robustness of reviewer identity both increase, this will spur contributors to push forward those parties closer to the actual use or performance being evaluated. As the system evolves, the data will become more accessible, more analysis will be completed on it, and more utility will be realized by a wider group of current and future potential users. As more parties find more uses for the system and its contents, the community of users and reviewers will expand. The Amazon product review system provides two interesting examples of this expansion: Many users post reviews on Amazon even after having purchased the product from another vendor entirely, and many reviewers not only indicate how long they have been using the product but return later to update their reviews after more use has occurred.

Additionally, as cycle time is reduced, an element of reducing cycle time will be highlighted, namely the direct input of information into a single system. The act of reducing cycle time through more direct access will lead to broader direct participation and more parties with the ability to directly contribute to various aspects of the reviews and responses included in the system.

MORE INTERACTION BETWEEN BUYERS, SELLERS, AND INTERESTED PARTIES

As access increases and the identity of participants becomes more robust, there will naturally occur an increase in interaction between buyers, sellers, and other interested parties. A current example of this is increased interaction between policymakers, program managers, firms, and industry groups as each of these endeavor to improve the utility, fairness, and utilization of the system. Industry groups have hosted forums and panels intended to increase collaboration and interaction on the system. Government policymakers have engaged and are making improvements. Agencies are raising the bar on past performance evaluation comments and completion of reports, which means increased interaction with contractors over the content of those reports. Although this increased interaction is currently taking place outside the system, meaning interested parties talk about and work together on ways to improve the system more than they interact within the system, increased interaction will arise in the form of collaboration between buyers and sellers within the system, specific to improving contractor performance, providing feedback to contractors, and making more informed source selection decisions.

MORE PROMINENT USE OF SOCIAL RESPONSIBILITY METRICS

The government has long stood out as a buyer that places more emphasis than most (until recently) on who the seller is. One impetus for change is the rise in concern for social responsibility and other contractor performance metrics. Many of these metrics can, are, and will increasingly be captured in past performance information system entries. Additionally, the rubber meets the road on performance against social responsibility metrics during contract performance. Therefore, the logical place to capture this performance data is during contract performance in the same way that information on subcontracting performance is collected in CPARS reports now. In the future, increased environmental impact concerns and heightened awareness of issues that fall under the broad categories of social responsibility and sustainability will become increasingly important, and these social and other responsibility metrics will rise in importance in systems of past performance evaluation and information retention.

PAST PERFORMANCE AS A TRUE INDICATOR OF FUTURE PERFORMANCE

Increased vigilance and more robust past performance monitoring can contribute to increased awareness and understanding of the implications of government policies from a micro to a macro perspective. For example, with the requisite capabilities in a past performance information system, the impact of setting aside procurements for specific socioeconomic categories on contract performance over a range of contracts could be determined down to fairly specific areas of performance, depending upon what aspects of performance are evaluated and recorded in the system. As another example, given the requisite system capability, past performance evaluation during source selection could be juxtaposed with contract performance evaluation as a step toward truly understanding the correlation between past and future performance.

Increased vigilance and more robust past performance monitoring and analysis can and should also lead us to question—and validate, if possible—the belief that past performance provides a reliable indicator of future performance. Is this potentially a falsehood or in some way misleading or leading the government to leave alternative—and potentially more effective—approaches off the table? Perhaps the government believes in past performance in the same way that it believes in competition as a cure-all (as embodied in countless regulatory policies, despite numerous academic studies that show otherwise), and because the government leads and defines its marketplace, others in that marketplace will just have to live with the fact that past performance will always be an evaluation criterion.

REFERENCES

Alliant Techsystems, Inc. v. United States, 178 F.3d 1260, 1268 (Fed. Cir. 1999), 41 GC ¶ 308.

Beausoleil, J.W. 2010. *Past Performance Handbook: Applying Commercial Practices to Federal Procurement.* Vienna, VA: Management Concepts.

Chapelle, H.I. 1949. *The American Sailing Navy: The Ships and Their Development.* New York: Konecky & Konecky.

Cohn, M. 2004. *User Stories Applied: For Agile Software Development.* Boston: Addison-Wesley.

Department of Defense Inspector General. 2008. *Contractor Past Performance Information.* D-2008-057. Available at http://www.dodig.mil/Audit/reports/fy08/08-057.pdf.

Edwards, V. 1995. *How to Evaluate Past Performance: A Best Value Approach.* Washington, DC: The George Washington University.

Edwards, V. 2005. *Source Selection Answer Book.* Vienna, VA: Management Concepts Press.

Garner, B., ed. 2009. *Black's Law Dictionary.* 9th ed. San Francisco: West Publishing.

General Services Administration. 2006. Proposed Best Practices Guide for Contractor Performance Data Collection and Use. 71 *Federal Register* 66782 (November 16, 2006). Available at http://www.gpo.gov/fdsys/pkg/FR-2006-11-16/html/E6-19392.htm.

General Services Administration. 2014. Mission Oriented Business Integrated Services (MOBIS), Solicitation Number TFTP-MC-000874-B, Description: 02 – Solicitation. Available at https://

www.fbo.gov/index?s=opportunity&mode=form&id=dd22037
189ac0fc2ba9fb06bb4b8f485&tab=core&_cview=1.

Goldstein, J., Hazy, J., and Lichtenstein, B. 2010. *Complexity and the Nexus of Leadership: Leveraging Nonlinear Science to Create Ecologies of Innovation*. New York: Palgrave Macmillan.

Government Accountability Office. 2009. *Federal Contractors: Better Performance Information Needed to Support Agency Contract Award Decisions*. GAO-09-374. Available at http://www.gao. gov/new.items/d09374.pdf.

Government Accountability Office. 2013. *Contractor Performance: DoD Actions to Improve the Reporting of Past Performance Information*. GAO-13-589. Available at http://www.gao.gov/ assets/660/655594.pdf.

Heskett, J., Sasser, W., and Schlesinger, L. 1997. *The Service Profit Chain: How Leading Companies Link Profit and Growth to Loyalty, Satisfaction and Value*. New York: Simon & Schuster, Inc.

Hogarth, R. 2001. *Educating Intuition*. Chicago: University of Chicago Press.

Manuel, K.M., and Schwartz, M. 2011. *GAO Bid Protests: An Overview of Time Frames and Procedures*. Congressional Research Service: http://fas.org/sgp/crs/misc/R40228.pdf.

Nagle, J. 1992. *A History of Government Contracting*. Washington, DC: The George Washington University.

Nash, R., Schooner, S., and O'Brien, K. 1998. *The Government Contracts Reference Book: A Comprehensive Guide to the Language of Procurement*. Arlington, VA: George Washington University.

National Performance Review. 1997. *Serving the American Public: Best Practices in Performance Measurement*. Available at http://

govinfo.library.unt.edu/npr/library/papers/benchmrk/nprbook.
html.

Office of Federal Procurement Policy. 2000. *Best Practices for
Collecting and Using Current and Past Performance Information.*
Available at http://www.whitehouse.gov/omb/best_practice_
re_past_perf.

Office of Federal Procurement Policy. 2011. *Improving Contractor
Past Performance Assessments: Summary of the Office of Federal
Procurement Policy's Review, and Strategies for Improvement.*
Available at http://www.whitehouse.gov/sites/default/files/
omb/procurement/contract_perf/PastPerformanceMemo-21-
Jan-2011.pdf.

Roberts, B., and Berg, N. 2012. *Walmart: Key Insights and Practical
Lessons from the World's Largest Retailer.* Philadelphia: Kogan
Page Limited.

Tate, W., and Council of Supply Chain Management Professionals.
2013. *The Definitive Guide to Supply Management and
Procurement: Principles and Strategies for Establishing Efficient,
Effective, and Sustainable Supply Management Operations.*
Upper Saddle River, NJ: Pearson FT Press.

Todd Constr., L.P. v. United States, No. 2010-5166, 2011 WL 3796259
(Fed. Cir. Aug. 29, 2011), 53 GC ¶ 299 (Todd IV).

Under Secretary of Defense for Acquisition, Technology and
Logistics. 2013. *Memorandum: Should Cost Management in
Defense Acquisition.* Available at http://www.acq.osd.mil/docs/
USA003343-13%20signed%20memo.pdf.

Walmart. 2014. 2014 Annual Report. Available at http://cdn.
corporate.walmart.com/66/e5/9ff9a87445949173fde56316ac
5f/2014-annual-report.pdf.

Wheeler, M. 2013. *The Art of Negotiation.* New York: Simon & Schuster, Inc.

Whelan, J.W. 1992. *Federal Government Contracts: Cases and Material.* Mineola, NY: The Foundation Press.

ACRONYMS AND ABBREVIATIONS

ACASS	Architect-Engineer Contract Administration Support System
ADRA	Administrative Dispute Resolution Act
CAGE	Commercial and Government Entity
CCASS	Construction Contractor Appraisal Support System
CFDA	Catalog of Federal Domestic Assistance
CFR	Code of Federal Regulations
CICA	Competition in Contracting Act
CFC	Court of Federal Claims
COR	Contracting Officer's Representative
CPARs	Contractor Performance Assessment Reports
CPARS	Contractor Performance Assessment Reporting System
CPFF	Cost Plus Fixed Fee
CSCMP	Council of Supply Chain Management Professionals
DCMA	Defense Contract Management Agency
DoD	Department of Defense
DRFP	Draft Request for Proposal
DUNS	Data Universal Numbering System
eSRS	Electronic Subcontracting Reporting System
FAI	Federal Acquisition Institute
FAR	Federal Acquisition Regulations
FAPIIS	Federal Awardee Performance and Integrity Information System
FCCX	Federal Cloud Credential Exchange
FFATA	Federal Funding Accountability and Transparency Act
FFP	Firm Fixed Price

FSC	Federal Supply Code
GAO	Government Accountability Office
GSA	General Services Administration
HUBZone	Historically Underutilized Business Zone
IAE	Integrated Award Environment
MAS	Multiple Award Schedule
NASA	National Aeronautics and Space Agency
OFPP	Office of Federal Procurement Policy
ORI	Open Ratings, Inc.
POC	Point of Contact
PPAQ	Past Performance Assessment Questionnaire
PPIRS	Past Performance Information Retrieval System
PPQ	Past Performance Questionnaire
PWS	Performance Work Statement
RCFC	Rules of the United States Court of Federal Claims
RFP	Request for Proposals
SAM	System for Award Management
T&M	Time and Material

GLOSSARY

Agency: A component of the government

Award fee plan: A plan developed and used by a government agency to administer the fee that a contractor receives (the award fee) above the base fee in a cost plus award fee contract.

Close at hand observation: Relevant (past performance) information in an agency's possession notwithstanding whether it was actually submitted by an offeror (see GAO B-401679.4 et al., Shaw-Parsons Infrastructure Recovery Consultants, LLC, and Vanguard Recovery Assistance, Joint Venture, 2010).

Bidder: A party that submits a bid; a prospective seller. A party bidding on a prospective (government) contract.

Business unit: A sub-unit of a firm or company.

Buyer: The party acquiring a good or services, typically the government or a government agency.

Company: A business entity that bids on and performs on government contracts or otherwise sells products and services. Synonymous with "firm" and "contractor" in most cases.

Contractor: A business entity under contract to provide products or services to a buyer. Synonymous with "firm" and "company" in most cases.

Debriefing: An explanation by an agency or buyer to a bidder or offeror of why it did not win a contract award.

Disagreement: Any differences in position between a contractor and the government on past performance issues, ratings, evaluations, decisions, etc., including situations that are correctly classifiable as either a dispute or a protest.

Discovery: The process of obtaining and the disclosure of information and evidence that the other party to a pending (legal) action has or intends to use.

Dispute: A disagreement between a contractor and a contracting officer regarding the rights of the parties under a contract (Garner, 2009).

Experience: The type and amount of work that a firm, person, or other business entity has completed.

Evaluation factor: Factors used by a buyer (a government agency) to assess the merits of offeror proposals in competitive procurements.

Firm: A business entity that bids on and performs on government contracts or otherwise sells products and services. Synonymous with "company" and "contractor" in most cases.

Government: The U.S. government; the agencies and departments of the government in general.

Key persons: "Contractor personnel that are required to be used in the performance of a contract by a Key Personnel clause" (Nash et al., 1998).

Offeror: Prospective contractor that has submitted or will submit a bid or a proposal. "The party that makes an offer and looks for acceptance from the offeree (i.e., seller)" (Garner, 2009).

Oral presentation: "A presentation by an offeror during source selection usually in lieu of submission of a written technical proposal, to demonstrate its capability to perform a proposed contract" (Nash et al., 1998).

Past performance: A composite of: (1) observations of the historical facts of a company's work experience—what work it did, when and where it did it, whom it did it for, and what methods it used; (2) qualitative judgments about the breadth, depth, and relevance of that experience based on those observations; and (3) qualitative judgments about how well the company performed, also based on those observations. (Edwards, 1995).

Performance: How well a firm, person, or other business entity has performed.

Privity of contract: An exclusive legal relationship between parties to a contract, including all rights and responsibilities under the contract.

Proposal: The offer submitted by an offeror in a negotiated procurement or other submission used as a basis for defining and pricing a contract, contract modification, or settlement, or to secure payments (see FAR part 15 and 31.001).

Protest: An "objection, submitted by an interested party in writing, protesting an agency solicitation for offers, the cancellation of a solicitation, or the award or proposed award of a contract" (Nash et al., 1998).

Requirement owner: The party or parties responsible for government program execution, at least enough to be responsible for accomplishment of a particular scope of work.

Responsibility determination: An instance where a government agency (i.e., a contracting officer) makes an affirmative determination that a contractor is an acceptable contract awardee.

Section L: The "Instructions, conditions, and notices to offerors or quoters" section of a solicitation under the standardized format of the Uniform Contract Format (which the government typically uses). This section describes what an offeror is to submit in a proposal and how it is to submit it.

Section M: The "Evaluation factors for award" section of a solicitation under the standardized format of the Uniform Contract Format (which the government typically uses). This section describes the evaluation scheme, evaluation factors and subfactors, and their relative importance. In plainer language; what the buyer will evaluate and how the buyer will evaluate it.

Seller: The party selling goods or services. Typically a firm or in some cases a person. A bidder or an offeror is a prospective seller.

Source selection: The process of determining which offeror to choose to make a contract award to among a group of offerors or other alternatives.

Statement of work: Used as a generic term in this volume encompassing statements of work, statements of objectives, performance work statements, or other articulations of a requirement or scope of a contract.

Venue: A forum where an appeal (e.g., of a decision regarding a past performance evaluation or other related decision) can be made.

INDEX